RAGS OF LIGHT

Short Theological Engagements with Popular Music

Series Editor: Christian Scharen

Editorial Committee: Margarita Simon Guillory, Jeff Keuss, Mary McDonough, Myles Werntz, Daniel White Hodge

Short Theological Engagements with Popular Music features theologians who have a passion for particular popular artists and who offer robust theological engagements with the work of that artist—engaging a song, an album, or a whole body of work over a career. Books in the series are accessible, yet deep both in their theological and musical engagement. Each book foregrounds ideas of interest in the musician's work, first, and puts these into conversation with the context and culture, second, and the Christian tradition, third. Each book, therefore, includes analysis of the cultural artifact, cultural context, and the relation to Christian tradition. Each book endeavors, as well, to speak with vitality to the challenges of living with God's mercy and justice in today's world.

RAGS OF LIGHT

*Leonard Cohen and the Landscape
of Biblical Imagination*

BRIAN J. WALSH

foreword by

J. Richard Middleton

CASCADE Books • Eugene, Oregon

RAGS OF LIGHT
Leonard Cohen and the Landscape of Biblical Imagination

Copyright © 2024 Brian J. Walsh. All rights reserved. Except for brief quotations in critical publications or reviews, no part of this book may be reproduced in any manner without prior written permission from the publisher. Write: Permissions, Wipf and Stock Publishers, 199 W. 8th Ave., Suite 3, Eugene, OR 97401.

Cascade Books
An Imprint of Wipf and Stock Publishers
199 W. 8th Ave., Suite 3
Eugene, OR 97401

www.wipfandstock.com

PAPERBACK ISBN: 978-1-6667-8213-4
HARDCOVER ISBN: 978-1-6667-8214-1
EBOOK ISBN: 978-1-6667-8215-8

Cataloguing-in-Publication data:

Names: Walsh, Brian J., author. | Middleton, J. Richard, foreword.

Title: Rags of light : Leonard Cohen and the landscape of biblical imagination / Brian J. Walsh; foreword by J. Richard Middleton.

Description: Eugene, OR: Cascade Books, 2024 | Short Theological Engagements with Popular Music | Includes bibliographical references and index.

Identifiers: ISBN 978-1-6667-8213-4 (paperback) | ISBN 978-1-6667-8214-1 (hardcover) | ISBN 978-1-6667-8215-8 (ebook)

Subjects: LCSH: Cohen, Leonard, 1934–2016. | Theology.

Classification: PR9199.3.C57 W40 2024 (paperback) | PR9199.C57 (ebook)

VERSION NUMBER 10/22/24

Unless otherwise indicated, Scripture quotations are from the New Revised Standard Version of the Bible, copyright © 1989, by the Division of Christian Education of the National Council of the Churches of Christ in the United States of America.

For Sylvia

"Raise a tent of shelter now
though every thread is torn.
Dance me to the end of love."

Contents

Foreword by J. Richard Middleton | ix

Preface | xvii

Chapter 1	You think maybe you will trust him: Cohen and the Promise of Jesus	1
Chapter 2	Lover, Lover, Come Back to Me: Cohen and the Biblical Landscape of Covenant	28
Chapter 3	When they said "Repent," I wondered what they meant: Cohen and the Prophetic Voice	70
Chapter 4	If it be your will: Cohen and the Priestly Calling	113

Postscript: "You Want it Darker" | 147

Discography of Leonard Cohen | 157

Films about Leonard Cohen | 160

Bibliography | 161

Song Index | 165

Poetry Index | 167

Scripture Index | 169

Foreword

J. Richard Middleton

I owe an immense debt of gratitude to Brian Walsh—both for this amazing book and for his impact on my life.

I first met Brian when we were graduate students together at the Institute for Christian Studies (ICS) in Toronto in the late nineteen seventies. I was a newly arrived immigrant from Jamaica and Brian got me my first speaking gig in Canada. Although I had done a lot of speaking at churches and youth groups in Jamaica, I had no connections in Canadian circles. Brian graciously suggested my name to the leaders of a Korean campus ministry group at the University of Toronto. I gave a talk for the group during my very first year in Canada.[1]

---

1. A few years later, I led a weekend retreat for the same Korean campus ministry group. It turns out that Christians in South Korea have had a long-standing interest in our work on the Bible and culture. Every book that Brian and I have written (together or separately) has been translated into Korean. Most recently (2023), I traveled to Korea to give two keynote lectures on a Christian worldview at the International Network for Christian Higher Education (INCHE) conference for Asia and Oceania, at Handong Global

FOREWORD

The next year Brian invited me to teach worldview courses for undergraduate students at the University of Toronto and McMaster University; these courses, which addressed the relationship of the vision of the Scriptures to our contemporary culture, were sponsored by Inter-Varsity Christian Fellowship, through an outreach program of the ICS that Brian directed. I was one of a number of ICS graduate students that Brian hired to teach in the program.

After a few years of teaching these courses, Brian suggested that he and I turn our course material into a book; the outcome was *The Transforming Vision* (published by InterVarsity Press in 1984). Some years later, we decided that we wanted to update the book to address the problem of suffering and the postmodern condition; but Rodney Clapp, our editor at IVP (who shepherded this book on Cohen to publication), suggested we write an entirely new book. The result was *Truth Is Stranger than It Used to Be: Biblical Faith in a Postmodern Age* (IVP, 1995).

Even before we began writing together, Brian and I were using music in our courses—especially the music of Bruce Cockburn. We both have been profoundly shaped by Cockburn's musical vision. I was first exposed to Cockburn through a live performance of "In the Falling Dark" by Peter Tigchelaar at the ICS during my first year in Canada. The following summer, I saw my first Cockburn concert at Ontario Place, Toronto. Being a born and bred Torontonian, Brian knew Cockburn's music long before that.

During the late eighties and nineties, Brian and I teamed up to do a number of joint presentations on Cockburn's musical vision, at McMaster University, the

---

University, Pohang, South Korea.

FOREWORD

University of Waterloo, York University, and the Festival of Faith and Writing at Calvin University. We also team-taught two short courses on Cockburn open to the general public in Toronto. A joint presentation that we did on Cockburn for the Canadian Theological Society was subsequently published as an academic article, "Theology at the Rim of a Broken Wheel."[2]

These joint speaking and writing projects were greatly enriching for me. But it was our team-teaching of a number of graduate courses at the ICS, especially a year-long course on the entire sweep of the biblical narrative (with a special focus on Jeremiah), that had the most lasting impact on my sense of vocation (we, of course, engaged lots of music in the course). Working side by side with Brian allowed me to see a master teacher at work. Brian modeled for me a passionate commitment to Christ and the Scriptures along with a pastoral heart for those he was teaching and a sharp, critical discernment of the idolatries of Western society.

Although he was never a formal mentor, and our personalities are different in significant ways (he's an extrovert, I am an introvert), I have learned an immense amount from Brian about being a minister of the gospel of Jesus Christ in the context of a church and world that need serious challenge and gracious healing. At one point in my journey I completed a self-study questionnaire, attempting to understand my own sense of calling and ministry. One of the questions asked me to reflect on the most important models or mentors in my life. Brian was at the top of the list.

---

2. Middleton and Walsh, "Theology at the Rim of a Broken Wheel."

FOREWORD

I want to acknowledge that it was Brian Walsh—by his inviting me to teach worldview courses and by his teaming up with me to write *The Transforming Vision*—that launched me on the trajectory of my academic career. Without Brian's graciousness and his energy, and his (implicit) mentoring over the years, I don't know where I would be today.

One of the differences between Brian and myself is our disciplinary orientation. Although we both started out as generalists in the theological field, after a stint in philosophy, I became a biblical scholar (with focus on the Old Testament), while Brian's formal academic focus was the theology of culture. When Brian and I began working together, my knowledge of the Bible outstripped his. Those days are long gone. Brian has become a superb interpreter of Scripture in his own right. I, on the other hand, have barely been able to keep up with his level of cultural analysis (indeed, I am not really close).

Although we have both used Cockburn's music in our teaching and writing, Brian devoted an entire book to Cockburn's musical vision, called *Kicking at the Darkness: Bruce Cockburn and the Christian Imagination* (Brazos, 2011). And now we have this masterful exploration of the vision of Leonard Cohen.

I haven't had the same relationship with the music and poetry of Leonard Cohen that Brian has had. If I have a musical specialization, it would be Bob Marley and the Wailers (Peter Tosh and Bunny Wailer), along with other classic reggae artists, such as Burning Spear, Toots Hibbert, Jimmy Cliff, Jacob Miller, and especially Third World (I went to high school with two of the founding members of the band).[3]

---

3. I regularly use Bob Marley's music in teaching, both for its

FOREWORD

Brian notes that the first Cohen song he ever seriously engaged was "Suzanne." It turns out that this was the first Cohen song I ever heard (while in Jamaica), through Neil Diamond's cover on his album *Stones* (1971). It wasn't till after I came to Canada that I was exposed to much Leonard Cohen. I started listening to Cohen seriously with the release of his 1992 album *The Future*. I often use the album's title song (in connection with Nietzsche's parable of the madman, as Brian also does) as a way to open up discussion of contemporary culture in courses that I regularly teach.

More recently, I have been drawn to "You Want It Darker," the title track on the last album released before Cohen's death in 2016.[4] Brian insightfully (and I think, correctly) connects the song to the call of Moses, who responds to God, as Cohen does in the song, with "Hineni" (Hebrew for "Here I am"). Brian's linking "We kill the flame" with the burning bush is nothing short of brilliant. I learned a great deal from Brian's nuanced interaction with so many of Cohen's songs, and this is no exception.

But I was personally struck by how "You Want It Darker" also echoed and amplified themes relevant to the binding of Isaac in Genesis 22 (something Brian doesn't address). Brian does note that both Moses and Abraham have the same response of "Hineni" to God's call (he lists every Old Testament character who responds with this word).[5] But perhaps because I listened repeatedly to the

---

resonance with biblical themes and to introduce students to the spirituality of reggae. For some of my analysis, see Middleton, "Identity and Subversion in Babylon."

4. There was a posthumous album, *Thanks for the Dance*, released in 2019.

5. Brian also mentions the two places (both in Isaiah) where God responds to us with "Hineni" (Isaiah 43:18–19; 58:6–9a). The

song while I was working on *Abraham's Silence* (my book on Genesis 22), I noticed that the line that came before "We kill the flame" was "You want it darker." This suggested to me that our killing the flame is not just a reference to human covenantal disobedience, our failure to live up to God's call (Brian's point); it could be alluding to Abraham's (attempted) obedience to the dark command that God gave him to kill his own son. No wonder Cohen sings, "I didn't know I had permission/To murder and to maim."

The slightly different resonance the song had with me illustrates Brian's own point that he isn't attempting to give a definitive interpretation of Cohen's poetry in this book. All great literature, especially poetry, has an intrinsic ambiguity that can never be finally captured by any one interpreter. Brian does a wonderful job of guarding, indeed, enhancing the beautifully evocative nuance of Cohen's lyrics, while exploring possible meanings that can help us reflect on the meaning of our lives in this complex, suffering world.

Brian's explicit project in the book (evident in his subtitle, *Leonard Cohen and the Landscape of Biblical Imagination*) is to put Cohen and Scripture into conversation, while bringing to bear both his own experience and the cultural and spiritual struggles of contemporary life—and see what happens.

---

translation Brian uses for the first of these is the Tree of Life (Messianic Jewish) translation, since it renders Hineni quite literally as "Here I am." In an amazing coincidence (or is it serendipity?), this is the very translation I take to church on Sunday mornings, just to defamiliarize myself from the standard renderings of more traditional English versions (it often replaces English words with their Hebrew equivalents: *Adonai* for Lord, *Ruach* for Spirit, etc.).

FOREWORD

What happens is a revelation. When Cohen's personal, honest, tender, yet flawed yearning for God (his cold and broken hallelujah) is illuminated by Brian's serious theological and pastoral engagement, the result is a book that has its own evocative, poetic vision and message. I've read every book Brian has written. This one has seared itself into my soul.

Be very careful. This book is dangerous. If you don't want to be deeply affected, you shouldn't read further. But if you are ready to open your (broken) heart to the Love at the heart of the universe, then, in the words of St. Augustine, *Tolle lege* (take up and read)!

WORKS CITED

Middleton, J. Richard. "Identity and Subversion in Babylon: Strategies for 'Resisting Against the System' in the Music of Bob Marley and the Wailers." In *Religion, Culture and Tradition in the Caribbean*, edited by Hemchand Gossai and N. Samuel Murrell, 181–204. New York: St. Martin's, 2000.

Middleton, J. Richard, and Brian J. Walsh. "Theology at the Rim of a Broken Wheel: Bruce Cockburn and Christian Faith in a Postmodern World." *Grail: An Ecumenical Journal* 9.2 (1993) 15–39.

Preface

His reputation is legendary. An insatiable womanizer, yet a man of prayer. A poet, a shepherd, a seducer and escape artist. A child of covenant who breaks the bonds of Torah. A man of beguiling contradictions, and yet millions have found such deep wisdom, faith, piety, and inspiration from this composer of psalms, writer of songs.

Who am I talking about? Well, it could be King David, or it could be Leonard Cohen. The author of so many of the psalms was deeply flawed, just as the composer of "Hallelujah" confesses to having received living waters, but holding them in stagnant pools. David and Leonard both wrote psalms of praise and lament, thanksgiving and complaint. And both continue to speak, whether from three thousand years ago, or thirty, or seven. So what happens if we engage them both? Or, more accurately, what happens if we read and listen to Cohen while bringing his work into conversation with David's psalms, Isaiah's prophecy, and that other prophet, priest, and king from small-town Nazareth? For Leonard had an ongoing relationship with Jesus that can be traced from "Suzanne" right through to "It seemed a better way" on the album that came out weeks before his death. So what happens if we allow Leonard to be a contemporary magi, offering his gifts of wisdom, tarnished from the journey, into our life of faith, our journey of doubt, our experiences of lament and joy, grief and hope?

We are not going to try to "figure out" Leonard Cohen. Nor is this an exercise in elucidating the theology or the worldview of Leonard Cohen. If there is a theology to be found in these pages, it is one of my own theological imagination as it emerges out of the interface of Cohen's songs, Scripture, and my own life in ministry in the twenty-first century. It is also important to say that I do not presume to offer any final or authoritative interpretations of his songs or poems. Indeed, some of my interpretations do not even address every verse in a song or a poem. No, my goal is more modest and perhaps more fun. We are going to bring Cohen and Scripture together within the context of our present cultural realities and spiritual struggles and see what happens. Cohen's work was crafted within the landscape of a biblical imagination. If we read Cohen in light of Scripture, and read Scripture in light of Cohen, might that creative engagement shed light on our own lives and the conflicted landscape in which we live?

While my engagement with Cohen goes back to high school, my conversation with his body of work deepened in the context of liturgy. In the Wine Before Breakfast community that I pastored from 2001 to 2020, we found ourselves frequently turning to Cohen to bring depth and contemporary voice to our prayers, our lament, and our praise. This community first met one week after the devastating attacks of September 11, 2001. As a result, we launched a new worshipping community not with happy praise songs, but in deep, deep lament. During our lament in that service we prayed these lines from "If it be your will."

> And draw us near
> and bind us tight,
> all your children here
> in their rags of light;
> in our rags of light
> all dressed to kill;
> and end this night
> if it be your will.

We knew that we were wearing rags of light, and yet in our anger and pain we were all dressed to kill. And so we prayed for the ending of this night, a way forward, a path of hope and healing. Such pathos became one of the defining features of the Wine Before Breakfast worship community. My spirituality has been profoundly shaped by my life with that community over some twenty years.

Over time, as Cohen's songs and prayers became almost a second language in our midst, we began to shape whole liturgies around Cohen's work. My co-conspirators in the shaping of these events were David Krause and Deb Whalen-Blaize. With the biblical texts assigned for a particular date in hand, and the whole catalog of Cohen before us, we would read and pray, listen and discern, until a creative and powerful liturgy emerged. Those were the most creative moments of my life as a campus minister at the University of Toronto. My debt to Dave and Deb is deep and profound.

The shape of this present book comes from a series of lectures called "If It Be Your Will: Epiphany and the Wisdom of Leonard Cohen." Hosted by the online educational community Bible Remixed, this course gathered fifty participants to listen to and reflect upon the songs and prayers of Cohen.[6] I am indebted to that community

---

6. https://www.bibleremixed.ca/.

PREFACE

of learners and to Bible Remixed for the impetus to write this book.

I am honored to have this book in the "Short Theological Engagements with Popular Music" series, edited by Christian Scharen. I have admired Christian's work on U2 and think that his book *Broken Hallelujahs: Why Popular Music Matters to Those Seeking God* is about the best introduction to this area of discourse that I know of. It is wonderful to be included in Christian's larger project.

Some of my most creative experiences engaging in theological interpretation of popular music have been with my friend and co-author, Richard Middleton. I am so pleased that Richard agreed to write a foreword to this book. He knows Cohen well, and he knows me better. Thank you, dear brother.

Rodney Clapp is my editor at Cascade Books on this project and it is always a good thing to work with my good friend. In one way or another, this is the seventh book that we have worked on together, with three different publishing companies. The venue might change from time to time, but Rodney is a mainstay in my publishing life. Emily Groen juggled a busy life with three children at home to give this manuscript a first edit that corrected many errors and grammatical infelicities. Sylvia Keesmaat also read the manuscript with a careful eye. I am so grateful to both Emily and Sylvia.

My children, Jubal, Madeleine, and Finn, were raised with the music of Leonard Cohen in the household and their father quoting lines from the growing body of his work. My partner, Sylvia Keesmaat, proves to me that Cohen is right in singing that "there ain't no cure for love," and so this book is gratefully dedicated to her. In times such as these may we "raise a tent of shelter now, though every thread is torn. Dance me to the end of love."

CHAPTER 1

You think maybe you will trust him

Cohen and the Promise of Jesus

What happens if we approach Leonard Cohen as something of a contemporary magi? It is, I admit, a bit of a stretch because the magi were, after all, dignitaries, wise men, soothsayers that came from the East. They came in fulfillment of the promise to Abraham that the light of Israel will shine amongst the nations. But those promises of light were not just about Israel, they were also *to* Israel. It is to Israel in the ruins of their culture that Isaiah proclaims:

> Arise, shine for your light has come
> and the glory of the Lord has risen upon you.
> For darkness shall cover the earth,
> and thick darkness the peoples;
> but the Lord will arise upon you,
> and his glory shall come to your light,
> and kings to the brightness of your dawn.
> (Isaiah 60:1–3)

PRAYING IN THE DARK

Few would contest the suggestion that as a poet, novelist, songwriter, and performer, Leonard Cohen has plumbed the depths of Isaiah's "thick darkness" throughout his career, both deeply within himself and the darkness that permeate the affairs of humanity in history and culture. Yet somehow the light has got in through the cracks, through the fissures, through the pervasive brokenness that Cohen has chronicled. So maybe Cohen can function for us as some sort of postmodern Magi, bringing gifts, and maybe even shedding a little light in the thick darkness of our time and our lives.

Both Isaiah and Leonard knew, however, that such darkness cannot be faced alone. There is no heroic individualism to be found in the work of Leonard Cohen. No sense that by some feat of human ingenuity, some strategy of civilizational progress, we can produce light. As we will see in this book, Leonard Cohen is a decidedly post-secular artist, eschewing the naive optimism born of the Enlightenment. If there is light to be found, it will be received in grace, received as gift. So it is not surprising that Cohen, always deeply tied to his own Jewish tradition, engages in his art within the context of prayer. In so many of his songs and poems we meet an artist struggling with his faith and contending with his God, as he seeks wisdom in a world of folly, faithfulness in the face of doubt, and healing in the midst of brokenness.

I suggest that if we are to engage Leonard Cohen theologically, indeed, if we are to seek to navigate our lives in the midst of deep darkness in conversation with Cohen, then we should follow his lead and do so in prayer. I'm proposing that we join Leonard in prayer as we seek to walk with him on the path of spiritual discernment, faith and doubt, joy and lament. No theology can happen apart from prayer, and, thankfully, Cohen has provided us with prayers that can spiritually ground and direct our exploration of his work. Throughout this book, therefore, we will dip into Cohen's 1984 work *Book of Mercy*, adapting his psalms into prayer litanies for our journey. In this adaptation of Cohen's psalm 43 from that book, I have set up the prayer responsively. If used in a group setting such as a study group or a church service, the italicized words are the responses of the community.

Let us pray.

> Holy is your name, holy is your work,
> *holy are the days that return to you.*
>
> Holy are the hands that are raised to you,
> *and the weeping that is wept to you.*
>
> Holy is the fire between your will and ours,
> *in which we are refined.*
>
> Holy is that which is unredeemed,
> *covered with your patience.*
>
> Holy, and shining with great light,
> *is every living thing,*
> established in this world and covered with time,
> *until your name is praised forever.*
>
> Holy is your name, holy is your work,
> *holy are the days that return to you.*[1]

---

1. Cohen, *Book of Mercy*, 43.

ON INTERPRETING COHEN

Towards the end of his poem "All My News," in his *Book of Longing*, Cohen writes:

> Undeciphered,
> let my song
> rewire circuits
> wired wrong,
>
> and with my jingle
> in your brain
> allow the Bridge
> to arch again.[2]

Taking the poet's advice, our interpretations in this book will not purport to decipher, in any final or exhaustive way, the meaning of Cohen's songs. Rather, we will let Cohen's art jingle in our brains. We'll listen for the resonance between Cohen's songs and our own journeys, and we'll set these songs in conversation with the very Scriptures that Cohen knew so well.

Earlier in "All My News" the poet writes:

> Do not decode
> these cries of mine—
> They are the road,
> and not the sign.

A poem or a song works when it opens up the world to us, when it accompanies us along the road and helps us to see more clearly, to experience more deeply. Art is an imaginative exercise in disclosure, the unfolding of our experience through careful attention. But this is not art for art's sake. No, this is art for healing, art to transform the imagination.

2. Cohen, *Book of Longing*, 42–43.

Closer to the beginning of this poem, Cohen writes that the purpose of his art was not to gain renown . . .

> but in the future
> some may find
> what might be used
> to change a mind
>
> from slaughter
> in the name of peace,
> to honouring
> complexities

Art to change the mind. Art for transformation. Art that honors complexities.

I'm excited to have this conversation with you, the reader, and the work of Leonard Cohen. But just a little scared—or perhaps intimidated—by the sheer scope, depth, and, indeed, complexity of it all. I know, and I suspect that you know, the power of Cohen's art. We all know how important his work has been to millions of people around the world. In the presence of these songs, people have experienced moments of healing, illumination, inspiration, and delight. Somehow, in the depths of the human sorrow and complicity to which Cohen bears eloquent witness, we find ourselves known. Something deep within us is touched when we are in the presence of this man's artistry.

HUNGER IN THE ROOM

Let me tell you a story.

I used to pastor a community at the University of Toronto called Wine Before Breakfast. In October 2012 the Wine Before Breakfast band and I led our first rock

Eucharist featuring the music of Leonard Cohen at the Church of the Redeemer in Toronto. The place was packed, and we really didn't know where most of these people had come from. They seemed to have been drawn to this church on that evening by something more powerful than simply wanting to hear renditions of some of their favorite Cohen songs.

The band started to play:

> Dance me to your beauty
> with a burning violin
> Dance me through the panic
> till I'm gathered safely in
> Lift me like an olive branch
> and be my homeward dove
> Dance me to the end of love[3]

I was in the front row with the rest of the congregation behind me. But I could tell, both from the faces of the musicians and from a feeling of intensity in the room, that as the song unfolded something was going on. Something else was transpiring beyond the enjoyment of beloved music. There was a clear mood, a force, indeed a "spirit" in the room. When the song ended and we all stood for the opening invocation, I turned around to look at the congregation.

What I saw was hunger. We had a church full of folks, many of whom had not graced a church door for a very long time, if ever, and they were all hungry. You could see it in their eyes, you could feel it in the space. The music of Leonard Cohen had awakened their hunger,

---

3. Cohen, "Dance Me to the End of Love," in *Stranger Music*, 337–38.

and somehow they thought that maybe engaging this artist in the context of a church might be able to touch that hunger.

I have met a similar reaction to Cohen in worship services, classes, and lectures over the years. There is a lot at stake for those who listen closely to the music of Leonard Cohen. This music and poetry matters to his fans, and I suspect it matters to you if you are reading this book. It matters to me too.

I also find it remarkable that this response to Cohen is so decidedly cross-generational. That night at the Church of the Redeemer we had a multigenerational full house. This was also the case in Cohen's late-in-life tours from 2008 to 2012, where audiences ranged from teenagers to their grandparents. Whether you were fourteen or eighty-four, there was something profoundly life-shaping going on with that old man on the stage with his fedora and amazing band.

When our family went to the Toronto show in 2012, our youngest child, Finn, was fourteen. And as we were walking through the venue to find our seats, Finn said,

"Wait a minute, isn't this where Justin Bieber played last night?"

"Yep, this is the place," I replied.

"On the same stage where Leonard Cohen will perform tonight?"

"Yep, same stage."

"That is just wrong," replied Finn, with disgust.

As far as this fourteen-year-old was concerned, Bieber couldn't hold a candle to Leonard Cohen.

SNAKES AND SUZANNES

The first song that we will be exploring is also the first of Cohen's songs that I ever seriously engaged.

It was my senior year of high school. At the end of one English class, Mr. Welsh read to us D. H. Lawrence's poem "Snake." Now, there is nothing wrong with this poem. Exploring, as it does, a primordial fear of serpents, the poem raises important questions about education and cultural formation, and our place in creation. But, after that one reading, Mr. Welsh gave us an assignment: "Go home and write a Freudian analysis of this poem."

Up shot my hand.

"Walsh?"

No sir, I'm not doing that.

"Why not?"

Well, none of us really know anything about Freud, except that somehow he was all about sex, and I'm not really interested in thinking about a snake, often connected with sexual temptation, slithering into a hole. I mean, I think about sex enough without having to do it in English class.

It also needs to be said that I had become a Christian just two years before this all happened, and, since I was an enthusiastic convert, everyone in the school knew that I followed Jesus.

As testimony to what a good teacher Mr. Welsh was, he didn't dig in his heals and insist that I do this particular assignment. Instead he said, "Well, what poem would you like to write an essay on?" And without forethought or hesitation, I replied, "'Suzanne,' by Leonard Cohen." I don't know why. It could just as easily have been "Like a Rolling Stone" by Bob Dylan, or even a poem by T. S. Eliot or Lawrence Ferlinghetti, but it was "Suzanne" that immediately came to mind. And that high school essay set me on a path of theologically engaging contemporary song that has had a profound impact on my life. Thank you, Mr. Welsh.

As I look back at my eighteen-year-old self, choosing to write on "Suzanne," I have to admit that it was probably the second verse that was crucial: "Jesus was a sailor when he walked upon the water . . ." Using a well-known, popular song, I probably wanted to demonstrate the relevance of Jesus in my secular classroom. *You see! If Leonard Cohen can openly talk about Jesus on a record and in the concert hall, then so can I in the secular halls of Victoria Park Collegiate!*

But I think there was more to it than that. There was something about this song that captured the imagination, even before any interpretation of its meaning. Francis Mus puts it this way: "There is no explicit message floating on the surface, only a mood, a feeling, an impression, and it this that constitutes the strength of the song."[4] I think that is right. If there is a message—and I think that there is—it is not floating on the surface. You've got to dig for it, or perhaps a more apt metaphor would be you've got to dive deep to find it. But there is clearly "a mood, a feeling, an impression" to this song. There is something wonderfully alluring about the picture that the song sonically and literarily paints.

A mysterious woman leads you to her riverside home. She's half-crazy, but that is her appeal. Even the tea and oranges that she serves you are experienced as exotic, "all the way from China." Wearing "rags and feathers from Salvation Army counters," this mysterious woman can

---

4. Mus, *Demons*, 167.

open your eyes to what lies "among the garbage and the flowers." What's not to love about these images?

There I was, a hormonally driven young man, writing a paper on this song to avoid what appeared to be the cheap sexual innuendo of the assigned project, and what did I find but a woman leading a man "to her place by the river." This is a place where the man is invited to "spend the night beside her." But this man inexplicably comes to the strange realization that he has "no love to give her." Everything about this scene is sensual, it all seems to be leading to the erotic, it seems to be heading inevitably to the bed, but (rather uniquely for a Cohen song) it doesn't.

The imagery is rich and dense. The lines are open to a myriad of interpretations. And while I'm not interested in deciphering these words with any finality, let me suggest that the song uncovers a deeply embodied connection, an intimate sharing of consciousness that is profoundly erotic, but not sexual. The imagery is erotic in the sense of *eros* as a longing for the other. But this is, I suggest, a covenantal longing. This is, if you will, a deeper dimension of eros. A touching of body and mind, regardless of whether bodies end up touching bodies.

Another kind of connection is going on here; the intimacy is of another kind of lover. "She gets you on her wavelength," she draws you into her world, her consciousness, and lets the river answer. The poem invokes that moving, living body of water to testify to this deeper connection "that you've always been her lover." Because of this connection, because of the depth of this relationship, you want to be her companion on the journey of life, you want to let it all go and "travel blind," without control, without a plan or even a map. You know that she can trust you, and she knows that you are not a sexual predator in this relationship "because you've touched her perfect body with your mind."

It is also interesting to watch the pronouns in the three choruses of the original recording of "Suzanne" as well as in different performances of this song.[5] In the first chorus, Cohen sings,

> And you want to travel with her
> and you want to travel blind
> and you know she will trust you
> for you've touched her perfect body with your mind

The focus of the last two lines of the chorus is on how *she* will trust *you* because *you've* touched *her* perfect body with *your* mind. In the second verse, focusing on Jesus, the pronouns shift.

> And you want to travel with him
> and you want to travel blind
> and you think maybe you'll trust him
> for he's touched your perfect body with his mind

Now it is a matter of how *you* think maybe *you'll* trust *him*, for *he's* touched *your* perfect body with *his* mind. And then in the final chorus, now back to Suzanne, we find a reversal of the first chorus:

> And you want to travel with her
> and you want to travel blind
> and you know that you can trust her
> for she's touched your perfect body with her mind

---

5. Where there is discrepancy between the recorded version of a song, and the published lyrics, I will privilege the recording. In this instance, there are slight variations between the words of "Suzanne" on the album *Songs of Leonard Cohen,* 1967, and those printed in Cohen, *Stranger Music.*

Notice the reversals: *you* know, not she knows, but *you* know that *you* can trust *her*, for *she's* touched *your* perfect body with *her mind*.

Who is trusting whom? Whose body is touched by whose mind? Well, at least between Suzanne and the poet, the relationship is delightfully mutual. Each can trust because both can trust. There has been an intimacy of intimacies in this embodied touching of minds, this coming together on each other's wavelength.

Now I've got to tell you, for my eighteen-year-old heart, this was exactly what I longed for in an intimate relationship. Yes, my hormones wanted sex, but my *eros* was more deeply directed to this kind of connection, this kind of heart-to-heart, soul-to-soul intimacy.

And then, in this song, Cohen took me to the One in whom I had such longings so deeply fulfilled. Admittedly, this was no orthodox telling of the Jesus narrative, and the biblical reference to the walking on water story wasn't exactly as Cohen had portrayed it, but that only made the allusions all the richer. Here was a Jesus who watched for thirty years. Waiting for the right time "when only drowning men would see him." And while I was barely a man at the time, I knew about spiritual and emotional, indeed cultural, drowning. As a sixteen-year-old hanging out in the downtown core of Toronto, I felt like a drowning man. Barely keeping my head above water, swimming in the turbulent currents of the time, I had no way of knowing where the shore was, I was devoid of any secure place to stand. Frightened, confused, alienated, and lonely, it was like I saw a guy walking on water, a guy who was in the storm, in the midst of the crisis, perhaps even walking into the crisis of my life, and he invited me to come to him. "Only drowning men shall see him."

If you are secure on shore, secure in your traditions, secure in your understanding of the world, self-secure in your own accomplishments, you will not see Jesus. Rather, as this poet so insightfully observes, if you are to see Jesus, you've got to be a sailor on that stormy sea, you've got to be in the midst of the crisis, you've got to experience your life to be at stake.

But.

There is a radically transformative "but" at the end of the second verse of this song. "But he himself was broken." In Cohen's poetic imagination, Jesus succumbed to the brokenness of us all. He himself went under the waves. He himself was broken "long before the sky would open" (long before the ascension), "forsaken" (my God, my God, why hast thou forsaken me?), "almost human" (abandoned by God, so tragically mortal), "he sank beneath your wisdom like a stone." Only drowning people, only people who know their predicament, could see in this Jesus a way through the storm. For those who are self-secure in their secular, self-made, comfortable lives, such a Jesus who, walking on water, sinks beneath their so-called wisdom like a stone.

"Suzanne" was released in 1967 on *Songs of Leonard Cohen,* but anyone who had read Cohen's debut book of poems would not have been surprised at all by the appearance of Jesus in his first hit record. *Let Us Compare Mythologies,* published in 1956 when the poet was a mere twenty-one years old, is a collection of incredibly mature poems written precisely at the interface of Jewish and Christian faiths, with some nods to the Hellenistic traditions of the ancient Greeks.

Christ is all over this early collection of poems. One of the pieces entitled "Ballad" is nothing less than a meditation on the cross:

> The people knew something
> like a god had spoken
> and stared with fear
> at the nails they had driven[6]

The poem "Saviours" employs the "Roman sport of crucifixion" as a metaphor to tell the stories of Moses, David, and Job. "For Wilf and His House" reflects on the impugned guilt of Jews for the crucifixion.[7]

So when this young star on the Canadian poetry and literature scene bucked the heady secularism of the sixties with a verse about Jesus in his hit song "Suzanne," he was continuing a conversation that had been at the heart of his poetic imagination from the beginning. There is nothing "secular" about the work of Leonard Cohen. While those who refer to him as a secular saint are right in noting the way in which he is revered broadly across the culture, including amongst those who have no explicit "religious" beliefs, portraying Cohen as "secular" betrays a fundamental lack of understanding.[8] If anything, Cohen is a post-secular or even anti-secular poet and songwriter. Rejecting the emptiness of secularism from the beginning, Cohen's art has always been one of deep religious engagement and profound biblical allusion that drips with theological meaning and insight. And Jesus has always been in the conversation. Or perhaps we could say that Jesus has always been a party to the argument that

6. Cohen, *Let Us Compare Mythologies*, 31.

7. See also "City Christ" and "Song of Patience," in *Let Us Compare Mythologies*.

8. See Bilefsky, "Secular Saint?"

Leonard has had with God and with his own rich Jewish tradition.

Note that, as it is with all good conversations, indeed, all good arguments, there is nothing static or absolute going on in Cohen. Once you have an absolute, once you have a final answer, once there is no more dynamism in the relationship, the conversation is over and so is the argument. For Cohen, the conversation is dynamic, ongoing, still unfolding. Indeed, the very way in which the chorus to the second verse of "Suzanne" (and the third, for that matter) unfolds over time indicates an open conversation, an unfolding and changing relationship.

As I have already noted, in the original version of "Suzanne" Cohen sings that when it comes to one's desire to travel with Jesus "you think *maybe* you'll trust him." While this trust is, like the relationship with Suzanne, rooted in the connection that Jesus has made with "you," it is more tentative than the trust that can be given to Suzanne. "Maybe you'll trust him."

The trust is more secure, however, in subsequent performances over the years. In a 1993 concert Cohen sings, "and you *know he will find you*/for he's touched your perfect body/with his mind."[9] Notice the dramatically increased confidence in these lines. While you may be lost, "you know he will find you." The question of whether you will trust Jesus is transformed into a more certain knowledge. Similarly, on *Live in London* Cohen sings, "and you *know you can trust him*/for he's touched your perfect body/with his mind."[10] Here we have moved from "maybe you can trust him" to a much more secure profession of faith, "you *know* you can trust him."

9. "Suzanne," *Cohen Live*, 1994.
10. "Suzanne," *Live in London*, 2009.

I should be clear that I am not making an argument here about a progressive development in Cohen's relationship with Jesus or even for a progressive development in Cohen's body of work as a whole on any particular theme. The chronology is interesting, and we will see that the Jesus relationship has its nuances and changes throughout Cohen's career. But what I think is clear is that in this song, and indeed throughout his life, Leonard Cohen was always dealing with Jesus.

LEONARD AND JESUS

Once, when asked about his relationship to Jesus, Cohen had this to say:

> I'm very fond of Jesus Christ. He may be the most beautiful guy who walked the face of this earth. Any guy who says "Blessed are the poor, Blessed are the meek" has got to be a figure of unparalleled generosity and insight and madness . . . A man who declared himself to stand among the thieves, the prostitutes and the homeless. His position cannot be comprehended. It is an inhuman generosity. A generosity that would overthrow the world if it was embraced because nothing would weather that compassion. I'm not trying to alter the Jewish view of Jesus Christ. But to me, in spite of what I know about the history of legal Christianity, the figure of the man has touched me.[11]

---

11. Cited from Jim Devlin, *Leonard Cohen: In His Own Words*. Quote accessed online at https://allanshowalter.com/2019/04/19/any-guy-who-says-blessed-are-the-poor-blessed-are-the-meek-has-got-to-be-a-figure-of-unparallelled-generosity-and-insight-and-madness-leonard-cohen-on-jesus-christ/.

While "legal Christianity" has been a story of anti-Semitism, colonialism, and empire, Cohen discerns in the Jesus of the Sermon on the Mount an inhuman generosity that would overthrow the world if it was embraced. Why? Because nothing could weather that compassion. And in an online chat forum, this question was posed to Cohen:

> You have such vivid Christian imagery in many of your songs, and much of it is contrasted with the selfishness of the "modern" individual. I was wondering what's your take on the state of Christianity today?

To which Cohen replied:

> I don't really have a "take on the state of Christianity." But when I read your question, this answer came to mind: As I understand it, into the heart of every Christian, Christ comes, and Christ goes. When, by his Grace, the landscape of the heart becomes vast and deep and limitless, then Christ makes His abode in that graceful heart, and His Will prevails. The experience is recognized as Peace. In the absence of this experience much activity arises, divisions of every sort. Outside of the organizational enterprise, which some applaud and some mistrust, stands the figure of Jesus, nailed to a human predicament, summoning the heart to comprehend its own suffering by dissolving itself in a radical confession of hospitality.[12]

Clearly Leonard Cohen has more than a passing interest in Jesus. If he is "comparing mythologies," as the title of his first book of poetry suggests, this is not a matter of disinterested and neutral academic religious studies. Not

12. Cited in "Cohen on Christianity," accessed online at https://walkingthewalk.org.uk/cohen-on-christianity/

only is Cohen attracted to Jesus, not only does he find in Jesus something that resonates with his own Jewish faith, but his very identity, spirituality, and hope is somehow bound up with Jesus. But again, this is "outside of the organized enterprise," outside institutional Christianity. Cohen may be post-secular, but he harbors no nostalgia for the Christendom of the past.

Just as this noninstitutional, nonecclesiastical Jesus makes appearances in Cohen's earliest poetry and song, so we also discern allusions to Jesus throughout Cohen's body of work. Here are just a few examples.

In the song "Is This What You Wanted?" on the 1974 album *New Skin for the Old Ceremony*, Cohen sings, "You were the promise at dawn/I was the morning after/You were Jesus Christ, my Lord/I was the money lender." In "Here It Is," on the 2001 album *Ten New Songs,* we hear this reference to the crucifixion: "Here is your cross/your nails and your hill/and here is the love/that lists where it will." The resurrection becomes the motif in this verse from "The Land of Plenty," also on *Ten New Songs:* "For the millions in a prison/that wealth has set apart/for the Christ who has not risen/from the caverns of the heart." And in the retrospective reflections on the posthumously released "What Happens to the Heart" on the 2019 album *Thanks for the Dance,* the artist remembers, "I was always workin' steady but I never called it art/I got my shit together meeting Christ and reading Marx/it failed my little fire but it spread a dying spark/go tell the young Messiah what happens to the heart."

Perhaps the most profound understanding of Jesus, however, comes mid-career in the iconic song "Ain't No Cure for Love," on the 1988 album *I'm Your Man*. There is a woundedness to love, the poet sings. This woundedness cannot be healed by time, nor by satiation. There is an aching to love, it is like a habit "and I'll never get enough." We meet here an erotic longing in the fullest sense of the word. And whether we search the universe or get all the doctors working day and night, "they'll never ever find that cure for love/there ain't no drink no drug/(Ah tell them, angels)/there's nothing pure enough to be a cure for love." Nothing pure enough to be a cure for love. Except, perhaps, the very love of God.

For Cohen, there is something inescapable and incurable about love. Recalling what I said about eros when talking about "Suzanne," we are, if you will, *homo eroticus*. We are erotic creatures: our lives are characterized by an insatiable yearning, a longing for relationship. Like the children in the third verse of "Suzanne," we "are leaning out for love," and we "will lean that way forever." And while that eros is at the heart of human relationships, especially relationships of sexual intimacy ("I'm aching for you baby/I can't pretend I'm not/I need to see you naked/in your body and your thought"), it is also at the heart of our relationship to God. And that is where Cohen takes us in the remarkable final verse of this song, where he bears beautiful witness to the scope, depth, and pathos that is at the heart of the biblical story, which comes to its head in the cross of Christ.

His misgivings about "legal Christianity" notwithstanding, it is no accident that the poet describes encountering the sweetest voice he ever heard *in a church*. He had, after all, "no place else to go." This was the place of last hope, the last refuge. And in that lonely church, "the sweetest voice I ever heard/whispered to my soul/I don't need to be forgiven/for loving you so much/it's written in the scriptures/it's written there in blood/I even heard the angels declare it from above/there ain't no cure, there ain't no cure, there ain't no cure for love." Next to,

> Christ has died
> Christ has risen
> Christ will come again . . .

is there a more eloquent summary of the gospel than that? Here we meet an understanding of Jesus that is more profound than you will hear from most pulpits on a Sunday morning. Who is most wounded by love, but the Author, Creator, and Source of Love? Cohen here evokes the suffering of God that permeates the biblical narrative.[13] This is the heart of the Scriptures, it is written there in blood. And this suffering of God, clearly anticipating the cross of Jesus, declares that the Holy One does not need to be forgiven for such incurable love. Indeed, this love will result in nothing less than the shedding of the blood of this Lover of all lovers. Commenting on this verse, and explicitly noting that the reference is to Jesus, Cohen said in an interview, "If the wound of Jesus comes to express his love for mankind, then it will never heal."[14] From a Christian theological perspective, this is a breathtaking insight.

Themes of incarnation, the cross, and resurrection are all easily at home in Cohen's imagination from the earliest to the latest songs. Consider two songs from his 2012 album *Old Ideas.* "Show Me the Place" sounds like a prayer. Taking the stance of a slave of the Holy One, the supplicant, with his head "bending low," prays "Show me the place/Where you want your slave to go/Show me the place/I've forgotten, I don't know." Show me the place,

---

13. One of the most profound and paradigmatic studies on this theme remains Fretheim, *Suffering of God.*

14. Interview with Alberto Manzano, in Burger, ed., *Cohen on Cohen,* 220.

Holy One, where you bid me to serve. Show me the place, for I am suffering from spiritual amnesia. Then the song alludes to Easter morning: "Show me the place/Help me roll away the stone/Show me the place/I can't move this thing alone." Somehow, if this slave is to obey the Master, it will have something to do with resurrection, with life bursting forth from death. Like the women on their way to the tomb asking, "Who will roll away the stone for us?" (Mark 16:3), Cohen's slave asks the same question. This moment of resurrection is not something that humans can accomplish on their own. And then the song shifts the metaphor from resurrection to incarnation: "Show me the place/Where the Word became a man/Show me the place/Where the suffering began." Clearly echoing John's Gospel where Jesus is identified as the Word that has become flesh, Cohen evocatively identifies such incarnation, such divine taking on flesh, with divine suffering.

Leonard Cohen had a deep affinity with the prophet Isaiah. As a young man he would sit with his maternal grandfather, the great talmudic scholar Rabbi Klinitsky-Klein, and they would study Isaiah together. Cohen recounts that the elderly rabbi would read a passage, explain it in some depth, and then doze off. Suddenly reawakening, "He'd read it again with all the freshness of the first reading and he'd begin the explanation over again, so sometimes the whole evening would be spent on one or two lines."[15] Cohen's biographer Ira Nadel rightly comments that "the Book of Isaiah, with its combination of poetry and prose, punishment and redemption, remained a lasting influence on Cohen's work and forms

---

15. Michael Benazon, "Leonard Cohen of Montreal," [Interview], *Matrix* 23 (Fall 1986) 52. Cited by Nadel, *Various Positions*, 13.

one of several core texts for his literary and theological development."[16]

One wonders whether the startling image of the suffering servant of the Lord, "despised and rejected," "a man of suffering," the "despised" one, "wounded for our transgressions, crushed for our iniquities" found in Isaiah 53 (vs. 3–5), might have led Cohen to such a profound understanding of divine suffering. If "Show Me the Place" alludes to the suffering that is entailed when the Word becomes a man, then "Come Healing" on the same album identifies the place of that suffering. "The splinters that you carried/The cross you left behind/Come healing of the body/Come healing of the mind." Or as Isaiah puts it, "by his bruises we are healed" (Isaiah 53:5).

Jesus is a constant companion and prominent figure in Cohen's poetic imagination right up to his final album, *You Want it Darker*, released weeks before his death in 2016. The song "It Seemed the Better Way" sounds like a concluding appraisal, a final coming to terms with this Jesus. Echoing both the Sermon on the Mount where Jesus instructs his followers not to return evil for evil, but to turn the other cheek when they are struck by the ruling oppressors (Matthew 5:38–39), and Jesus's word to Martha that her sister, Mary, had chosen "the better way" of listening to Jesus rather than busying herself with domestic duties (Luke 10:42), Cohen opens the song by singing, "It seemed the better way/When first I heard him speak/Now it's much too late/To turn the other cheek." In this achingly beautiful song, the poet recalls choosing that better way, sitting at the feet of Jesus. He recalls being enamored by this radical call to turn the other cheek in the face of a culture and a cruel history of violence and

16. Nadel, *Various Positions*, 13.

genocide. He recalls the unparalleled generosity, madness, and insight that drew him to Jesus. But now, nearing the end of his life, the poet is having second thoughts. And so he invites the male choir of his home synagogue, Shaar Hashomayim, to join him, to hold acoustic space with him, to accompany him in this painful assessment of his path with Jesus. I remember weeping through this song when I first heard it. What once was appealing, what once seemed like the truth, what once seemed the better way, "is not the truth today."

While Cohen had already confessed years earlier that "the staggering account of the Sermon on the Mount" was something that he didn't "pretend to understand at all,"[17] now he is resigned: "It's too late to turn the other cheek." Perhaps there are too many enemies. Perhaps there is animosity that is too deep in the chest. Perhaps the pacifism of Jesus has always been a stumbling block for this poet. Even the incurable love of Jesus, written in the Scriptures, inscribed on those pages in blood, even the powerful symbolism of the wounded one on the cross, all of which has been so alluring, so suggestive, so full of meaning, now leaves the artist wondering. "I wonder what it was/I wonder what it meant/At first he touched on love/But then he touched on death." It made sense once. It seemed the better way. He talked about love and manifested that love in death. Love and death always go together. "For God so loved the world that he gave his only son" (John 3:16). "Greater love has no man, but to lay down his life for his friends" (John 16:13). Somehow, all of that made sense, but it doesn't make sense now.

I suspect that most of us who are drawn to the spirituality, to the struggle and authenticity of Leonard Cohen,

---

17. "Democracy," *Stranger Music*, 367.

including—if not especially—those of us who come to Cohen from a place of Christian faith, can deeply relate to the poet's struggle with Jesus. That's probably why we find such a spiritual kinship with Cohen. This dance of faith and doubt, of being deeply attracted to Jesus and yet having serious second thoughts, is where many of us have been at various points in our lives. What seemed the better way, what seemed like the truth, what had moved from "maybe you'll trust him" to "you know you can trust him," has lost its appeal, and you aren't at all sure that this story of Jesus is your story, so you are left with an anxious sense of loss. What do you do? Well, consider the stunning last verse of "It Seemed a Better Way."

> I better hold my tongue
> I better take my place
> Lift this glass of blood
> Try to say the grace

Holding his tongue, the poet understands his place and adopts a stance of humility, rather than an arrogant militance against Jesus. Yes, there is deep doubt, ambivalence, and struggle here, but the poet does not close the door on Jesus. Rather, he brings together the shocking image of lifting a glass of blood with the Jewish tradition of saying a grace, a thanksgiving, to the Lord of the Universe after a meal. This is a clear and provocative reference to the Eucharist.

In the midst of profound questioning and doubt, concluding that this comparison of mythologies has gone on long enough, considering that the "better way" of Jesus might not be the truth today, the poet, nonetheless, reaches for the eucharistic cup, and then will try, as difficult and impossible as it seems, to say the Hebrew grace at the end of it all. This break-up song of break-up songs still ends up at table together. The fracture of the relationship still comes together in communion. But can warring factions share table fellowship? Can there be a Jewish prayer of thanksgiving for a Christian Eucharist? Now that we are no longer "comparing mythologies" but living in the tension, in the crisis, in the dissolution of mythology or even, perhaps, the war of mythologies, a burning question lingers. Is there a treaty, a truce, that can be achieved?

"Treaty" is a song of spiritual exhaustion in which there is still a longing, but it is tempered by despair. "I wish there was a treaty we could sign/I do not care who takes this bloody hill/I'm angry and I'm tired all the time/I wish there was a treaty/I wish there was a treaty/Between your love and mine." The pathos of this song is heartbreaking. A child of the covenant, formed in the embrace of the faith, wishing there was a treaty that could be signed, when such a treaty, such a covenant has been at the heart of it all from the beginning. Yet, a treaty is needed, a new covenant, a truce to bring this argument to an end. A treaty to declare a truce in this war of the spirit, a treaty in this war of the wills that can heal his anger and bring peace between two lovers.

Of course the question that is so often asked of Cohen's songs is whether this is about a woman or God. And, more often than not, the answer is both. In Cohen's imagination the sacred and the sexual, spirituality and human intimacy, are so interrelated that it is difficult to separate them from each other. But what else would we expect from *homo eroticus*? What else would we expect from the defining role of eros in human life? As we have seen in our discussion of "Suzanne," the longing of eros for intimacy, for deep connection, indeed, for covenant, shapes all of human life.

In this song, however, I think that it is fair to say that the relationship with God is more foundational. Indeed, Cohen is still struggling with Jesus. The tip-off is in the first line of the song. "I seen you turn the water into wine." But this is no longer a wedding feast at Cana (John 2:1–2). Nor is this is a joyful celebration of intimacy, because "I try but I just don't get high with you." Rather, this relationship has collapsed into an exhausted anger: "I'm angry and I'm tired all the time." The relationship has dissolved into abandonment and deceit: "I haven't said a word since you've been gone/That any liar couldn't say as well." And while the dissolution of this relationship, the breaking of this covenant, might seem like liberation because "we sold ourselves for love but now we're free," the result has in fact been a confused disorientation. "I just can't believe the static coming on," he sings. You see, this lover, this one who changed the water into wine, functioned as a stable point of orientation for the poet: "You were my ground—my safe and sound/you were my aerial." The word is aerial, as in antenna. This is a radio metaphor. Without that aerial, all that can be received is static, and communication is broken down. Without that radio signal, there is not enough information to navigate the path ahead. This lover with whom there seems to be no treaty available, who was the poet's safe and sound, the very ground of this poet's being, seems finally lost. There is no treaty, there is no covenant.

At the very end of *You Want it Darker* we hear a "String Reprise" of "Treaty." A string quartet evocatively and achingly rehearses the tune for two and a half minutes. Then Leonard's voice returns one last time:

> I wish there was a treaty we could sign
> It's over now, the water and the wine

We were broken then, but now we're borderline
I wish there was a treaty
I wish there was a treaty
Between your love and mine

As we will see in the rest of this book, "brokenness" is a ubiquitous theme in Cohen's writing. There is a rupture in the world. There is betrayal at the heart of things. Wounded in every atom, this brokenness goes all the way down. But at the end, he confesses that we were broken then, but now we're borderline. I'm not sure of any way to interpret this apart from borderline personality disorder. I am not arguing that this is a matter of the artist engaging in some kind of psychological self-diagnosis; rather, I suggest that Cohen is offering both a cultural and theological diagnosis. Once we were broken and struggling to find healing, but now, as in borderline personality disorder, we are caught in a downward spiral of abandonment and rejection. As a cultural diagnosis, this sets off patterns of anger, lashing out, fear, impulsiveness, and self-absorbed narcissism. All of this was happening in American culture as Cohen was breathing his last. But this was also a theological diagnosis. Didn't the psalmist cry, "My God, my God, why have you forsaken me" (Psalm 22:1)? And didn't Jesus say the same thing on the cross (Matthew 27:46)?

"I wish there was a treaty we could sign," this child of the covenant laments. In the next chapter we will dive more deeply into the nature of this covenant, in the songs and poetry of Leonard Cohen.

CHAPTER 2

Lover, Lover, Come Back to Me

Cohen and the Biblical Landscape of Covenant

In 1984, a few months prior to the release of Cohen's seventh studio album, *Various Positions*, the poet published a collection of prayers titled *Book of Mercy*. One could interpret the two together as a diptych with *Book of Mercy* as the first panel and *Various Positions* as the second. Rabbi Mordechai Finley argues that with this book Cohen established himself as nothing less than "the greatest liturgist alive today."[1]

FAILED STRATEGIES AND DIVINE YIELDING

The first prayer or psalm of that collection begins . . .

> I stopped to listen, but he did not come. I began again with a sense of loss. As this sense deepened I heard him again. I stopped stopping and

1. Cited in Mus, *Demons*, 168.

> I stopped starting, and I allowed myself to be crushed by ignorance. This was a strategy, and didn't work at all.[2]

The intuition is right. Stop to listen. What else would a child of the covenant do? What else would one who recites the Shema do? "Hear O Israel." "Listen O Israel." People of Torah, people of the Word, your identity is constituted, grounded, and formed by listening.

So the postmodern psalmist stops to listen, with the amazing assumption that there is something to hear. But the hope of being addressed is denied. The Holy One does not come. In response to the absence in that silence the poet makes another move. He begins with loss. He begins with his own emptiness, his own spiritual need and longing. It is in this loss that the poet begins to hear. And he stays with the loss. He stops stopping and stops starting, and allows himself to be crushed by ignorance, to be humbled by what he does not know.

But this too was a strategy. This was still a matter of control, a machination of his own design. And such strategies, such attempts at control, have never worked for Cohen. Nonetheless, all he has are strategies. The psalm/poem continues: "Much time, years were wasted in such a minor mode. I bargain now. I offer buttons for his love. I beg for mercy."

The supplicant continues to pray. With hope against hope, he continues to engage in strategies and machinations of the spirit, even though he knows that they don't work. And then, slowly and haltingly, the Holy One responds:

> Slowly he yields. Haltingly he moves toward his throne. Reluctantly the angels grant to one

2. Cohen, *Book of Mercy*, 1.

> another permission to sing. In a transition so delicate it cannot be marked, the court is established on the beams of golden symmetry, and once again I am singing in the lower choirs, born fifty years ago to raise my voice this high, and no higher.[3]

While the artist knows that there are no "strategies" that can move the Creator of the Universe, he has nothing else to offer, he has no other recourse. And so, like the incessant widow in the parable of Jesus, the poet just keeps coming back.[4] He keeps pestering the Holy One, knowing that there is nothing he can offer to achieve the love of God, or to receive the Mercy, or to live in a state of Grace.

And yet . . . somehow, the Creator of the Universe yields. The Holy One returns to the throne from which he was exiled. The Divine Mind is changed. God repents.

While such a thing is impossible in the Christian imagination of an immutable, eternally unchanging, absolute God, for this Jewish poet, living within the landscape of a covenantal imagination, it makes total sense that the Holy One can change and even repent. A God of covenant, a God who is in relation, is a God who can yield to our insistent prayers. Moreover, while the omnipotent, omniscient, and immutable God of traditional theology from the church fathers to today is a God who could never vacate the divine throne, in the more dynamic covenantal imagination of Israel, the God of covenant can be both exiled from the throne, leaving us as souls "without a king,"[5] and wooed back to the throne by our prayers.

---

3. Cohen, *Book of Mercy*, 1.
4. Luke 18:1–8.
5. Cohen, "Heart with No Companion," *Various Positions*.

The Holy One has been on the throne before, and things didn't go so well. No wonder the angels are reluctant to sing anew. They have borne witness to the breaking of the throne, the breaking of the heart of God. And yet, in the poet's imagination, the throne room, the heavenly court, is re-established "in a transition so delicate it cannot be marked," and the artist himself, the supplicant with his strategies, the one who longs to listen and to hear again the liberating Voice of the Word, is given his place as a singer in one of the lower choirs, to raise his voice "this high, and no higher."

Oh my goodness. That is so not rock and roll. That is in such profound tension with secularism. That is so incredibly beautiful, wise, and prayerful. And, as we saw in the first chapter of this book, there is a profound sense that in Cohen's body of work as a whole, but especially in an offering like *Book of Mercy,* we are being invited into prayer. This litany is a responsive adaptation of psalm 48 in that book of contemporary psalms.

AN AWAKENING PRAYER FROM THE DREAM OF DESPAIR

Let us pray:

> Awaken me, Lord, from the dream of despair,
> *and let me describe my sin.*
>
> Awaken me to the homeland of my heart
> *where you are worshipped forever.*
>
> Awaken me to the mercy of the breath,
> *which you breathe into me.*
>
> Remove your creature's self-created world,

and dwell in the days that are left to me.
Dissolve the lonely dream which is the
judgment of my ignorance,
and sweep aside the barricades of uncleanness,
which I commanded against the torrents of mercy.

Let your wisdom fill my solitude,
and from the ruin raise your understanding.
Blessed is the name of the glory of your kingdom
forever and forever.

What I have not said,
give me the courage to say.
What I have not done,
give me the will to do.

It is to you, and you alone who refines the heart,
you alone who instructs mortals,
who answers the trembling before you with wisdom.

Blessed is the name of the one
who keeps faith with those who sleep in the dust,
who has saved me again and again.

To you is the day, and the conscious night,
to you alone the only consecration.

Bind me, intimate,
bind me to your faithfulness.
Amen.

In this prayer there is a longing for homecoming, but not without a confession of the sin that resulted in exile. There is something powerfully honest about such a prayer. In the face of his despair, the supplicant seeks mercy. In this fatal predicament in which folks literally "can't breathe," we hear a prayer for the renewal of breath. There is no spirituality of escape here. No inclination to cover up despair and exile with sweetness and light. No averting our gaze from what's really gone wrong. No cheap hope and easy homecoming. This psalmist refuses to point anywhere beyond his own sin, and thereby demonstrates that there is no awakening without confession.

"Awaken me to the homeland of my heart," prays our psalmist. My heart is estranged; my heart is not at home within myself or my world, or with my Creator. And the poet knows that such awakening is impossible without mercy. If we look closely, however, we might notice that this is a mercy that has always been there, but we have missed it in our spiritual and cultural slumber. Indeed, this is a mercy that has been there from the beginning. It is as foundational as the breath we breathe, the very breath breathed into that creature fashioned out of the mud at our creation. As Genesis 2 tells the story, "Then the Lord God formed an earth creature out of the earth [a human from the humus, 'adam from the 'adamah], and breathed the breath of God into this earth creature, so that the earth creature became a living being."[6] And so any prayer for homecoming is a prayer that returns to the radical and generative grace of the homemaking Creator who has primordial mud on the divine hands and lips.

Recognizing that our exile is from the goodness of creation into the machinations of our own autonomous constructions, Cohen's prayer appropriately turns more deeply into petition:

> Remove your creature's self-created world,
> and dwell in the days that are left to me.
> Dissolve the lonely dream which is the
> judgement of my ignorance,

6. Genesis 2:6 (replacing "Adam" with "earth creature").

and sweep aside the barricades of uncleanness,
which I commanded against the torrents of mercy.
Let your wisdom fill my solitude,
and from the ruin raise your understanding.

This self-created world, this world of arrogant human autonomy, is a world in the ruins of ignorance and foolishness, in which we have fallen asleep in the lonely dream of broken covenant. And only the covenant-keeping God, only the God of steadfast love and faithfulness, can refine the heart and instruct in wisdom those who come trembling before the throne. We are trembling in this dream of despair because it is a nightmare. Rather than blessing the dust of our birth, we are sleeping in the dust of death. And so we long for the homecoming of resurrection, bound anew in faithful intimacy to our Creator.

Our contemporary psalmist confesses that it is this Creator God alone who refines the heart, instructs us in wisdom, keeps faith. The Holy One is the God of salvation, who keeps covenant. And, remarkably, this artist who has always struggled with the bonds of commitment, this poet of seduction and fleeing, awakened anew before the God of covenant, asks to be bound in covenant. "Bind me, intimate/Bind me to your faithfulness."

Here we meet a surrender of the will together with an acknowledgment that faithfulness is at the heart of things. Whispering through the end of this prayer, there is a deep realization that precisely because we are incurable covenant-breakers, we are unable, on our own moral strength, to bind ourselves in covenant. Mr. Cohen speaks from extensive personal experience. Since we do not have the moral character to bind ourselves by our own will to covenant, we need the Holy One to bind us in covenantal intimacy. We have here a God who yields . . . faithfully. Indeed, this is a God who will yield in mercy because faithfulness and steadfast love require it. Or we could simply say again that "there ain't no cure for love," especially the love of God that is the foundation of all things. And without that incurable love meeting our habitual homebreaking, there can be no homecoming.

A BIBLICAL LANDSCAPE

Of course, all of this is to employ a deeply biblical vocabulary. A few centuries of modernity have left us either with no such vocabulary to help us address the deeper questions, or—perhaps worse—a blasphemous bastardization of that vocabulary. Nonetheless, Cohen lives in and invites others to find themselves dwelling within what he calls the biblical landscape. The failure to understand that landscape results in interpretations of Cohen's work that are often banal, resolutely avoiding any engagement of the rich theology that resonates through Cohen's most profound work.

Christian Raab's insightful article "Leonard Cohen's Biblical Vision" is a notable exception. He cites a 1993 interview in which Cohen reflects on Jewish survival and inhabiting a biblical landscape:

> I know what it takes to survive. I know what a people needs to survive and as I get older I feel less modest about taking these positions because I realize we are the ones who wrote the Bible. And, at our best, we inhabit a biblical landscape, and this is where we should situate ourselves without apology. For these things, for the burning bush . . . those are the experiences that we have the obligation to manifest. That

> biblical landscape is our urgent invitation, and we have to be there. Otherwise, it's really not worth saving or manifesting or redeeming anything, unless we really take up that invitation to walk onto that biblical landscape.[7]

Without apology, Cohen invites us to inhabit a biblical landscape, to manifest and to walk our days in that landscape. This is, he confesses, our urgent invitation. Here is the literary, metaphorical, and spiritual key to the imaginary of Leonard Cohen. This is the grand narrative in which his art lives. Here is the beating heart of his poetry and song, even when those poems and songs, together with his life, are in deep tension with that landscape. Recall that this is, after all, a landscape populated by scoundrels and broken people, driven by selfishness and violence. Just like Leonard. Just like us. And so, in this chapter, we are going to walk through that biblical landscape, and tell the biblical story, with Mr. Cohen as our tour guide.

REVISITING JESUS AND SUZANNE

But first, we must return to "Suzanne." Somehow, Cohen couldn't tell the story of Suzanne apart from the story of Jesus, and we spent a fair bit of time in the first chapter of this book on the second verse of Cohen's famous song. But the third verse was left hanging, and that is no way to leave such an iconic song.

> Now Suzanne takes your hand
> And she leads you to the river
> She is wearing rags and feathers
> From Salvation Army counters

7. Quoted by Raab, "Cohen's Biblical Vision."

> And the sun pours down like honey
> On our lady of the harbour
> And she shows you where to look
> Amid the garbage and the flowers
> There are heroes in the seaweed
> There are children in the morning
> They are leaning out for love
> And they will lean that way forever
> While Suzanne holds the mirror
>
> And you want to travel with her
> And you want to travel blind
> And you know she will trust you
> For she's touched your perfect body with her mind.[8]

As we have already seen, from the beginning this song is about the depths of human connection, echoed by creation in the river, the water, the sun, the seaweed. It is a song about trust, and just as the chorus to the second verse changes in different performances, so have the words varied in the third chorus over the years. On *Live in London,* the artist sings, "and you know she will trust you/for she's touched your perfect body with her mind." But the original 1967 lyrics are "and you know that you can trust her/for she's touched your perfect body with her mind."[9] In the 1993 Vancouver concert, Cohen sang, "and you know that she will find you/for she's touched your perfect body with her mind."[10] And in the 2013 concert in Dublin, the lyrics were "and you know you will find her/for she's touched your perfect body with her mind."[11]

---

8. Cohen, *Live in London.*
9. Cohen, *Songs of Leonard Cohen.*
10. Cohen, *Cohen Live.*
11. Cohen, *Live in Dublin.*

We see in these various performances of "Suzanne" a delightful dance between who can trust who, indeed who can "find" who. The shifting pronouns simply bear witness to the lovely mutuality of it all. There is an intimate relationality in this song, and it has something to do with the touching of minds and perfect bodies. But this is no idealized Western notion of perfect bodies, the likes of which Cohen will so vehemently attack in "First We Take Manhattan." Rather, I suggest that these "perfect bodies" are a vision of our bodies, our lives, as can be imagined in the eyes of a lover; indeed, as we are imagined in the eyes of God. Jesus and Suzanne can both see us as we truly are, as we are most authentically called to be: Beloved. And that is why we want to travel with them, that is why there is an openness here to a deep trust, a deep finding of oneself in relation to another.

While Jesus is a sailor in his lonely wooden tower, waiting to take your hand once you realize that you are drowning, Suzanne takes your hand now—perhaps because she sees that you are drowning, though you don't see it yourself—and leads you to the river. This figure of salvation, this lady of the harbor, shows you where to look amid the garbage and the flowers. She helps you to see your way through the waste and the beauty. If you look close enough, you will find strength and courage in the most unlikely places, with these "heroes in the seaweed." And, most poignantly, you will see the children, and "they are leaning out for love/they will lean that way forever/ while Suzanne holds the mirror."

As Cohen will sing many years later, "love's the only engine of survival."[12] The creature that I described in the last chapter as *homo eroticus* is the creature that

12. Cohen, "The Future," *Stranger Music*, 371.

is born in love, created in love, called in love, fulfilled in love, and therefore will always lean out and towards love. We will lean that way forever, while Suzanne holds the mirror. Suzanne, like Jesus, and I suggest, like the biblical narrative, holds a mirror that reflects to us who we really are. Bringing together the metaphor of the mirror with the touching of perfect bodies with minds, Lisa Warenski writes, "To touch someone's perfect body is, among other things, to play the role of the magical mirror, the mirror that reflects not only what is but what can be."[13] I suggest that Cohen engages the landscape of a biblical imagination as precisely such a mirror reflecting not only what is but what can be. This is a magical mirror, if you will, that provides us miraculously with not just a vision *of* the world, but also *for* the world.

WALKING THROUGH THE BIBLICAL LANDSCAPE WITH COHEN

For the rest of this chapter we will explore that scriptural landscape, tracing its song lines, through the song and poetry of Mr. Cohen. I begin with some key images shaping the biblical imagination:

> *Genesis 1:1–2, 3*
> In the beginning, when God created the heavens and the earth,
> the earth was a formless void
> and darkness covered the face of the deep . . .
>
> Then God said, "Let there be light,"
> and there was light . . .

---

13. Warenski, "Mystery of the Mirror," in Holt, ed., *Cohen and Philosophy*, 112.

and it was good.

It was good,
it was good,
it was good.
Delightful.
Very good.

Psalm 33:4–9

The Word of the Lord is upright,
and all God's work is done in faithfulness.
The Holy One loves righteousness and justice;
the earth is full of the steadfast love of God.

By the word of the Lord the heavens were made,
and all their host by the breath of God's mouth.
The Creator gathered the waters of the sea in a bottle;
and put the deeps in storehouses.

Let all the earth fear the Lord;
let all the inhabitants of the world stand in awe.
For God spoke, and it came to be;
the Creator commanded, and it stood firm.

CREATION: FROM DELIGHT TO SORROW

Here is the most foundational thing to say about creation in the biblical landscape. The Holy One has created a good, delightful home of mutual interrelations overflowing with love. All things live in response to the calling, inviting, constituting Word of the Creator. All things are subjects, responding to this creational call. The "shema Israel," the call to covenantal listening, is rooted in the very foundations of the cosmos. All that exists is a response to a call. The grounding Torah injunction to love the Lord our God is reflective of the loving Voice that echoes throughout creation. Without listening to and heeding that Voice, there is no creation. In this primordial vision of the world, it is not so much a matter of *creatio ex nihilo,* creation out of nothing, as a *creatio per verbum,* creation by word. Or perhaps an even more evocative image would be *creatio per cantum*—that is, creation by song.[14]

This story, unlike all other origin myths of the ancient Near East, begins in delight and is grounded in love. But before long that ground cries out. The ground from which the earth creature is created becomes polluted by the violence of that very creature. Home is broken and all creation cries out in anguish.

> *Genesis 4:9–12*
>
> The Lord said to Cain, "Where is your brother Abel?"
> Cain replied, "I don't know; am I my brother's
>   keeper?"
> And the Lord said,
> "What have you done? Listen, your brother's blood
> is crying out to me from the ground!
> And now you are cursed from the ground . . .
> [which will] no longer yield to you its strength;
> you will be a fugitive and a wanderer on earth."

And so the earth which is good, good, good, the earth from which we are born, cries out as it is soaked in the blood of our violence, rendering us fugitives and wanderers, exiled from our creational home. No wonder, this all breaks the heart of God.

---

14. See Walsh, *Kicking at the Darkness*, 67–68.

Genesis 6:5–7

The Lord saw that the wickedness of humankind
was great in the earth,
and *every inclination of the thoughts of their hearts
was only evil continually.*
And the Lord *was sorry* that he had made humankind
   on the earth
and it *grieved God to his heart* . . .
I am sorry that I made them.

As the mutuality of love devolves into nothing but evil and violence, so the delight that the goodness of all things gave the Creator is now replaced with a devastating divine grief.

With these images in our minds, of a good creation defiled in blood and the broken heart of God, consider Cohen's waltz called "The Faith," from the little-known 2004 album *Dear Heather*. The biblical allusions in this song are rich and open to multiple interpretations. But what happens if we hear this song with the biblical language of Genesis and the vision of Psalm 33 resonating and echoing throughout?

> The sea so deep and blind
> The sun, the wild regret
> The club, the wheel, the mind,
> O love, aren't you tired yet?
> The club, the wheel, the mind
> O love, aren't you tired yet?

Is that sea, so deep and blind, the primordial waters of creation, dwelling in darkness? Might that sea be an anticipation of the flood that comes after the Creator's devastating grief, God's wild regret that he ever made humankind? And looking at the history of violence, with our primitive tools of clubs, wheels, and minds whose inclination is always to evil, isn't it worth asking whether it was all worth it? Doesn't the Creator consider such a devastating conclusion? If the earth is overflowing with the creating, calling, inviting, and life-giving love of God, then doesn't the devastating question need to be asked, O love aren't you tired yet?

> The blood, the soil, the faith
> These words you can't forget
> Your vow, your holy place
> O love, aren't you tired yet?
> The blood, the soil, the faith
> O love, aren't you tired yet?

And, with Abel's blood crying out from the soil, with the blood of the Holocaust, the blood of ethnic cleansing, the blood of the children, all soaked into the soil that is our life . . . indeed, the blood and soil that so demonically shapes our identities of nation and race wreaking such havoc in our history, don't we need to ask, O love, aren't you tired yet?

In the landscape of biblical faith, the Holy One has made a vow. The very word that called us into being was a vow, and after the flood, the grieved Creator, who was sorry that humankind was ever created, vows anew to never destroy the world in such a way again. But if love is tired, then might the vow be withdrawn, and all holy places left desecrated and abandoned?

> A cross on every hill
> A star, a minaret
> So many graves to fill
> O love, aren't you tired yet?
> So many graves to fill
> O love, aren't you tired yet?

And what about the ever-filling and overflowing graves of descendants of this Word, the recipients of this vow, this covenant? How long must this go on? Holy One, aren't you tired of all of this yet? Love, haven't your children pushed you to the limit? "So many graves to fill/O love, aren't you tired yet?"

> The sea so deep and blind
> Where still the sun must set
> And time itself unwind
> O love, aren't you tired yet?
> And time itself unwind
> O love, aren't you tired yet?

But what would it mean if love were to be tired? What would it mean if the love that is the very foundation of creation should come to its end? Wouldn't that mean the end of creation? The setting of the sun upon those primordial waters? The return to darkness and inactivity? Endless homelessness? The very unwinding of time?[15] We leave the question hanging.

COVENANT

As the story unfolds, it would have appeared that love was tired and had met its limit as early as Genesis 6. But the story is only beginning. There is so much more unfolding of God's love that is to come. It starts over, of course, with the covenant to Noah and all living things, after the flood.

> *Genesis 9:8–17*
>
> Then God said to Noah and to his sons with him, "As for me, I am establishing my covenant

---

15. la Terre, "An Interpretation of 'The Faith.'"

with you and your descendants after you, and with every living creature that is with you, the birds, the domestic animals, and every animal of the earth with you, as many as came out of the ark. I establish my covenant with you, that never again shall all flesh be cut off by the waters of a flood, and never again shall there be a flood to destroy the earth."

God said, "This is the sign of the covenant that I make between me and you and every living creature that is with you, for all future generations: I have set my bow in the clouds, and it shall be a sign of the covenant between me and the earth. When I bring clouds over the earth and the bow is seen in the clouds, I will remember my covenant that is between me and you and every living creature of all flesh; and the waters shall never again become a flood to destroy all flesh.

When the bow is in the clouds, I will see it and remember the everlasting covenant between God and every living creature of all flesh that is on the earth." God said to Noah, "This is the sign of the covenant that I have established between me and all flesh that is on the earth."

Covenant is at the heart of this story, and every path on this landscape is going somewhere in relation to covenant. Love makes covenant, even in the face of the faithlessness, violence, and evil of the beloved. And just as love goes all the way down—the earth is full of the steadfast love of God—so also is a covenantal worldview not limited to humans. Notice that the narrator of Genesis reminds us repeatedly that this covenant is not limited to Noah and his descendants, but is with the earth and every living creature. Perhaps that is why Cohen can sing, "If it be your will/If there is a choice/Let the rivers fill/Let the hills rejoice."[16] Or, "The river's going to weep/And the mountain's going to shout, 'Amen.'"[17]

You see, when a Jew, rooted in the biblical imagination, bears witness to creation weeping, shouting, singing, and rejoicing, there is more than anthropomorphism going on. This is not just the excess of poetic language. Such language is rooted in a creation born in love, bound in an intimate relation of covenant to the Creator. This, I suggest, is more foundational to the landscape of Jewish faith than the covenant with Abraham. Indeed, when the covenant is focused on one tribe, one people, the family of Abraham, that choosing of Abraham is intended to be a blessing to the whole earth. Abraham was to be a witness to what covenantal life looks like. The choosing of Abraham wasn't because of any unique virtue of this person (the evidence suggests that he was given to lying in service of self-preservation). Rather, in the face of the home-wrecking violence that continued to plague the earth after the flood, the Noahic covenant with all of creation and all of humanity finds a narrowing down to one family through whom the steadfast love of home with God and all of creation would be renewed.

THE BINDING OF ISAAC

Which is why the story of Isaac remains so controversial in both Judaism and Christian theology to this day. The subject of art, literature, and song throughout the ages, the story of God requiring Abraham to sacrifice his son,

16. Cohen, "If It Be Your Will," *Various Positions*.
17. Cohen, "Democracy," *The Future*.

Isaac, has been the center of debate and spiritual consternation throughout the history of its telling. How could the covenant God, desiring to make peaceable home with humanity in a good and delightful creation, ever require such a violent act of home-breaking?

> *Genesis 22:1–3*
>
> After these things God tested Abraham. He said to him, "Abraham!" And he said, "Here I am." He said, "Take your son, your only son Isaac, whom you love, and go to the land of Moriah and offer him there as a burnt offering on one of the mountains that I shall show you." So Abraham rose early in the morning, saddled his donkey, and took two of his young men with him and his son Isaac; he cut the wood for the burnt offering and set out and went to the place in the distance that God had shown him.

Take your son, your only son, and just in case there is any confusion, let's be clear that this is the son whom you love. Take this son, the son born to fulfill the covenant promise to Abraham and Sarah, the son on whom the redemption of not only the children of Abraham, but the whole world, rests . . . and make a sacrifice of him. Slaughter the boy, and burn his flesh.

The binding of Isaac, also known as the Aqedah, has put rabbis, scholars, theologians, and everyday believers in a bind for centuries. What do we do with a story that is so foundational to biblical faith when it calls for child sacrifice? What do we do with the God who we meet in this story, or, for that matter, the father of a child willing to obey such a God? In a recent book, *Abraham's Silence: The Binding of Isaac, the Suffering of Job, and How to Talk Back to God,* J. Richard Middleton offers a bold interpretation of this disturbing story. Setting his reading of Genesis 22 in the context of the tradition of lament psalms, the suffering of Job, and the biblical narrative of a covenantal God who not only can change, but also suffers, Middleton argues that Abraham actually *failed* the test set before him. While this is a man who has demonstrated a willingness to argue with God in the story of the destruction of Sodom (Genesis 22:18–33), when the Holy One demands the sacrifice of the son whom he loves, Abraham remains silent. And that silence, Middleton argues, was not a sign of deep faith. This was not a test that Abraham passed, but rather this was a failure of the test, a failure of faith, indeed, a failure of covenant. Abraham should have argued back with God, as he had at least partially argued on behalf of the inhabitants of Sodom when God was determined to destroy that city.

The test, or the question in this story is, "What kind of a God makes covenant, promises an heir, fulfills that promise, and then demands child sacrifice?" This is the question that Abraham did not ask. And by not asking that question, by not arguing with God about whether this order that he sacrifice his son was faithful, by not calling the covenantal God to be faithful to his covenant, Abraham allows the God of covenant to be reduced to the vindictive, child-sacrifice–demanding gods of the nations out of which he had been called.

I share with you Middleton's interpretation because Cohen offers a similar reading (or "midrash") of this disturbing tale in his song "Story of Isaac," from his 1969 album *Songs from a Room*. And in doing so, Cohen takes up his place amongst the rabbis. While the song has autobiographical overtones (Cohen was nine when his father died) and clear resonance with the anti-war movement of the late sixties, it is the interpretive daring that I find so striking. The song tells the story from Isaac's perspective:

> The door it opened slowly
> My father he came in
> I was nine years old
> And he stood so tall above me
> Blue eyes they were shining
> And his voice was very cold
>
> Said I've had a vision
> And you know I'm strong and holy
> I must do what I've been told
> So we started up the mountain
> I was running he was walking
> And his axe was made of gold

In a cold voice, the father announces that he has had a vision. And, insisting that he is both strong enough to carry out the vision and holy enough to be worthy of such a task, he tells his son that he must do as he is told.

The father's hand, however, tells a different story. On the way up the mountain, the father and son stop to drink some wine, "and he put his hand on mine." The hand that is to take the life of his son is placed lovingly on the child's hand. And the father's hand returns towards the end of the song. Addressing the contemporary listener to this tale, the narrator recounts, "You were not there before/ When I lay upon a mountain/And my father's hand was trembling/With the beauty of the word." The word that calls Abraham to such a deed may well be beautiful—to a Jew, what else could the word of God be?—and yet, that beauty somehow combined with the horror of the command leaves the father's hand trembling.

Initially the son is confused. "Thought I saw an eagle/But it might have been a vulture." What was that bird?

Was it an eagle? Will the boy rise up on eagle's wings? Is salvation from this tragedy at hand? Or is it a vulture? Is this a bird of carrion, come to strip the meat off his flesh? "I never could decide," declares the son. Cohen leaves the question hanging. Where was this story really going to end? Could this possibly be a salvation story? The story of a restored home? Or would the vultures come and clean up after the desolation of home, the betrayal of the covenant?

Of course, this is not just the story of Isaac, but the story of all Isaacs since. This is a story of all children born for calamity, born for sorrow. And so the song ends with the child passing his own judgment.

> You who build the altars now
> To sacrifice these children
> You must not do it anymore
> A scheme is not a vision
> You never have been tempted
> By a demon or a god

You called it a vision, but it was no more than a scheme. You called it a test, but the child will not allow the cheap escape of either "this is God's will" or "the devil made me do it." Not unlike Middleton's, it would seem that Cohen's telling of the story discerns that such a vision, such a demand, could only be a test of Abraham's understanding of what kind of a God he is dealing with. As Middleton suggests that Abraham should have argued with God, called God to be the covenantal God of life that had already been revealed, and not a vindictive deity of child sacrifice demanding unquestioning obedience, so Cohen insists that this scheme cannot be a true vision of the God of Abraham, Isaac, and Jacob. Calling for the end of child sacrifice, Cohen stands in the solid biblical tradition of the prophet Jeremiah:

> They have turned their backs to me, not their faces;
> though I have taught them persistently,
> they would not listen and accept correction.
> They set up their abominations in the house that bears
>   my name and defiled it.
> They built the high places of Baal in the valley of the
>   son of Hinnom,
> to offer up their sons and daughters to Molech,
> though I did not command them,
> *nor did it enter my mind* that they should do this
>   abomination,
> causing Judah to sin. (Jeremiah 32:33–35)

What were they thinking? How could the God of covenant, the God of faithfulness, be a god of child sacrifice? How could the God of a home-making covenant engage in such domicide, such murder of home? According to Jeremiah, the idea is so offensive that it takes the Holy One totally by surprise. Not in the deepest regrets of God's heart could such a thing ever be countenanced or imagined. And yet, what the Holy One couldn't have imagined, and what the poet/rabbi calls to be abolished, is something that clearly reflects the violent realities and compromised complicity of human affairs.

The song ends with honesty and a longing for mercy:

> When it all comes down to dust
> I will kill you if I must
> I will help you if I can
>
> When it all comes down to dust
> I will help you if I must
> I will kill you if I can
> Have mercy on our uniform

Man of peace or man of war
The peacock spreads his fan

Commenting on this song, Cohen once said:

> [The "Story of Isaac"] has fathers and sons in it and sacrifice and slaughter, and an extremely honest statement at the end. . . . The song doesn't end with a plea for peace. It doesn't end with a plea for sanity between the generations. It ends saying, "I'll kill you if I can, I will help you if I must, I will kill you if I must, I will help you if I can." That's all I can say about it.[18]

The song ends with an "extremely honest statement." However things unfold, whatever we must do, and whatever we can do, it doesn't matter: there will be help and there will be death, there will be death and there will be help. So what are we left with? A cry for mercy on all of us. Man of peace or man of war, really it is just a matter of perspective. All require mercy, for all are held captive by imaginations of violence.

And yet, "the peacock spreads his fan." What a perplexing concluding line. Is this an image of the all-seeing Holy One symbolically represented as the eyes of a spread peacock fan, before which no one can hide? Or might this be the machismo show of violent men, posing in all of their power and virility, scheming yet more violent conquest? Either way, Lord have mercy.

So what happened? What happened in this story of promise, so nearly thwarted? What happened to this family, that was to be a light to the nations? What happened to this father and son? Well, Abraham came down the mountain. Alone. He does not return to his servants

[18]. Interview with Robin Pike, in Burger, ed., *Cohen on Cohen*, 70.

with his son Isaac. Not surprisingly, father and son go their separate ways. How could they possibly continue together? After such a profoundly traumatic event, after coming so close to being murdered by his father, how could the son go back to "life as normal" in the family? The way the story goes in Genesis, Abraham comes down the mountain alone, and there is no record of Isaac seeing his father again until he came to bury him with his brother Ishmael in Genesis 25. Is it any surprise that the rest of Genesis is a sordid tale of a deeply dysfunctional family? Is it any surprise that out of the trauma of the Abraham/Isaac relationship there emerges a family of betrayal and deceit, violence and sexual predation? Where else could this tale go?

OUT OF EGYPT

If such a crucial storyline in this biblical landscape is one of family violence, is it any surprise that the story ends up not in the promised land of milk and honey, but the alien landscape of imperial Egypt? It all ends up, not as a free people living out the covenant in a promised land, but as an enslaved people subject to empire. The dream of covenant dissolves into the nightmare of Pharaoh. If there is to be a people of promise, if there is to be a reopening of this story after the dead end of Egypt, then there must be liberation from imperial bondage. And so the story of the exodus proves to be an even more important origin story than that of Abraham.

Exodus 2:23–25

> After a long time the king of Egypt died. The Israelites groaned under their slavery, and cried

> out. Out of the slavery their cry for help rose up to God. God heard their groaning, and God remembered his covenant with Abraham, Isaac, and Jacob. God looked upon the Israelites, and God took notice of them.

What else could be at the heart of a covenantal faith, what else could so profoundly shape the biblical landscape, but the story of the exodus?

While there has been lots of talk over the years about how long Leonard Cohen took to write "Hallelujah," it is in fact his song "Born in Chains" that he said took the longest.[19] Appropriately enough, Cohen worked on this song for forty years, which is how long the children of Israel were in their exodus wanderings in the wilderness. An earlier version under the title "Out of Egypt" was slated to appear on the 1984 *Various Positions* album, but it was deemed incomplete. The song was finally released on the *Popular Problems* album in 2014. Indwelling the story as his own, Cohen inserts himself into the narrative:

> I was born in chains
> But I was taken out of Egypt
> I was bound to a burden
> But the burden it was raised
> Lord, I can no longer
> Keep this secret
> Blessed is the name,
> The name be praised
>
> I fled to the edge
> Of the mighty sea of sorrow
> Pursued by the riders
> Of a cruel and dark regime
> But the waters parted

---

19. Cited by Showalter, "Stellar Video."

> And my soul crossed over
> Out of Egypt,
> Out of Pharaoh's dream

This is not a story just to be told about what happened to our ancestors millennia ago. No, this is a story that is to be our own. And so, Cohen tells it as his story. The bondage of Israel in Egypt, being caught up in Pharaoh's dark dream, the captivity, the chains, the burden . . . all of this is taken up into Cohen's self-understanding, all of this shapes the identity and forms the imagination of this poet. It was *his* soul that crossed over that mighty sea of sorrow. It was *his* burden that was raised.

And so the secret is out. The secret that secular modernism wants to keep hidden. The secret confession that is so embarrassing to the ears of self-secure secularism must now be sung in public: "Blessed is the Name/The Name be praised." Blessed by the unutterable Name of the Holy One. Blessed is the name revealed in the burning bush. Blessed is the name of the Faithful One. Blessed is the name of the Great I Am.

> Word of Words
> And Measure of all Measures
> Blessed is the name
> The name be blessed
> Written on my heart
> In burning letters
> That's all I know
> I cannot read the rest

In the face of a world in which "Things are going to slide in all directions/Won't be nothing/Nothing you can measure anymore,"[20] the artist bears witness to a measure of all measures. The word of life, the word of freedom, the

20. Cohen, "The Future," *Stranger Music*.

word of covenant, the word that calls all things into being, the word that comes as Torah to a sojourning wilderness people is the "Measure of all Measures." Echoing the prophet Jeremiah who experienced the word of the Lord as a fire burning in his heart (20:9), and who prophesied a return to covenant in which God's word will be written on our hearts (31:33), our poet confesses that this word has been written on his heart with burning letters. That's all he knows, but that is enough, even if he can't read the rest.

> I was idle with my soul
> When I heard that you could use me
> I followed very closely
> But my life remained the same
> But then you showed me
> Where you had been wounded
> In every atom
> Broken is the name

The gift of this Word of Words always comes with a calling both to service and transformation. Maybe that is why the word must be burned on our hearts. And maybe that burning cannot happen merely by listening. Maybe we need to be shown the wounds that we have inflicted on our covenantal Partner. You see, the word, the Torah, doesn't just prescribe a way of life (though it does that), it also reveals nothing less than the broken heart of God. Perhaps alluding to Jesus showing Thomas his wounds,[21] or maybe simply keying in to the theme of God's suffering that runs throughout Israel's story, the poet has seen where God has been wounded "in every atom, Broken is the Name." The brokenness of the cosmos is mirrored in the brokenness of God. The rupture, the fissure that

---

21. John 20:26–29.

breaks the unity and harmony of all things, renders the Name itself as broken.

> I was alone on the road
> Your love was so confusing
> All my teachers told me
> That I had myself to blame
> But in the Grip
> Of sensual illusion
> A sweet unknowing
> Unified the name

It is, of course, hard to see clearly in a world of such brokenness. You may have been freed from your chains, there may have been an exodus experience in your life, but that doesn't make it easy to live in such freedom. You may even have had Torah written on your heart, and found that measure of all measures, but it is still so easy to be disoriented, to lose your way.

So whose fault is this? The authorities say that you are to blame for your own confusion, but that seems too simple. Your sensuality seeks to find illumination and wisdom in eroticism, but that is an illusion that paradoxically only opens your eyes to what you don't know. But in that surrender to your ignorance, in that sweet unknowing, somehow things begin to come together; somehow the Name is unified, and the path is set again for the unification, the wholeness and healing, of all things.

TORAH

As we dwell in these rich images, we see that the unity of the Name, the coming together of all things, the repair of the breach, the healing of the brokenness, the restoration and sustaining of covenant, is all tied up with that Word of Words, Measure of all Measures. And so a scriptural landscape shaped by Torah will find the seeker in constant struggle with God's law. This is the opening verse and chorus of "The Law," from the 1984 album, *Various Positions:*

> How many times did you call me
> And I knew it was late
> I left everybody
> But I never went straight
> I don't claim to be guilty
> But I do understand
>
> There's a Law, there's an Arm, there's a Hand
> There's a Law, there's an Arm, there's a Hand

Throughout the Law and the Prophets, the phrase is repeated, "with a mighty hand and an outstretched arm the Lord brought you out of Egypt" (Deuteronomy 7:19). Embedded in the ten words of freedom, at the heart of the Ten Commandments, in the longest description of any of the commandments, in the call to keep sabbath, Torah declares:

Deuteronomy 5:15

> Remember that you were a slave in Egypt, and
> the Lord your God brought you out from there
> with a mighty hand and an outstretched arm;
> therefore the Lord your God commanded you
> to keep the sabbath day.

The outstretched arm and hand of God, mostly occurs in the Bible as a metaphor of deliverance, liberation, redemption, and loving care. The law is not a weapon. Torah is not a club with which to beat up others or to beat up on ourselves. It is never a matter of the Law being wielded in the arm and hand of God to punish evildoers. Cohen's song "The Law" understands that the Law is a calling and that he is late in responding. And while the artist knows that he falls short of this calling, he doesn't "claim to be guilty" because "Guilty's too grand." Nonetheless, he acknowledges that something is deeply wrong:

> Now the deal has been dirty
> Since dirty began
> I'm not asking for mercy
> Not from the man
> You just don't ask for mercy
> While you're still on the stand

There is an uncleanness here, an impurity at the heart of things. And when the fault runs that deep, there is no point in seeking mercy from "the man," from the authorities who portend to be the keepers, the guardians, of the law. Indeed, the poet understands that his rebellion, his quest for autonomy, his rejection of covenantal faithfulness has been met with nothing less than the justice of God. And yet, he also so beautifully grasps that where there is a law, there is always an arm of liberation, there is always a hand of healing, mercy, and redemption. Not surprisingly, such motifs recur in the book of Isaiah.

Isaiah 48:22

> Listen to me, O Jacob,
> and Israel, whom I called:
> I am He; I am the first,
> and I am the last.
>
> My hand laid the foundation of the earth,
> and my right hand spread out the heavens;
> when I summon them,
> they stand at attention.

The hand that laid the foundations of the earth and spread out the heavens, the right hand that summoned all of creation into being, the calling, loving, generative word of the Great I Am, the hand that got dirty forming the human from the humus, responds to Israel's guilt in the breaking of Torah by proclaiming:

> *Isaiah 51:16*
>
> I have hidden you in the shadow of my hand.
>
> *Isaiah 52:10*
> The Lord has bared his holy arm
> before the eyes of the nations;
> and all the ends of the earth shall see
> the salvation of our God.
>
> *Isaiah 66:14*
>
> You shall see, and your heart shall rejoice;
> your bodies will flourish like the grass;
> and it shall be known that the hand of the Lord
> is with his servants . . .

"There is a Law, there is an Arm, there is a Hand." This is not an ominous warning of judgment, but a liberating confession to the loving, healing, and merciful character of the covenant-making God who gives us the Torah.

RETURN TO COVENANT

Covenants are always tumultuous. Precisely because covenant is lived out in real time, in real history, with real struggles, temptations, betrayals, and anger, there is always a painful dynamic of leaving and returning, there is always home-breaking, exile, and the longing for return.

LOVER, LOVER, COME BACK TO ME

The story is always messy. No song rehearses the covenantal argument that has shaped the scriptural landscape and the covenantal imagination better than the dialogical "Lover, Lover, Lover" from the 1974 album *New Skin for the Old Ceremony*.

When Egypt and Syria attacked Israel in 1973 on Yom Kippur, the Day of Atonement, Cohen immediately left his home on Hydra and made his way to Tel Aviv. Once there he hooked up with a group of Israeli musicians and went to the front lines to perform for the troops. "Lover, Lover, Lover" was written in the context of war, but it is no Zionist rallying call. Rather than a nationalistic anthem blithely proclaiming "God is on our side, so we will surely prevail," the artist begins in cowardice.

> I asked my father,
> I said, "father change my name."
> The one I'm using now it's covered up
> With fear and filth and cowardice and shame.

Naming the cowardice and shame that was undoubtedly the experience of so many of the young soldiers thrown into this war, together with the sense of betrayal, and of not being worthy of the name of his ancestors, the song entreats the father to bestow upon the son a new name. The father replies by moving the metaphor from name to body.

> He said, "I locked you in this body,
> I meant it as a kind of trial.
> You can use it for a weapon,
> Or to make some woman smile."

Perhaps the metaphor needs to shift because it was what was done with these bodies, and perhaps what was done to other bodies, that has occasioned this crisis of shame.

The issue isn't to change your name, or even to escape your embodiment, but to determine what you will do with your body. Will you bring delight or death? This remains the covenantal question that goes all the way back to the "it is good, so delightful" that shapes the biblical landscape from the beginning in contrast to the grief, violence, and sorrow that so quickly followed.

> "then let me start again," I cried,
> "please let me start again,
> I want a face that's fair this time,
> I want a spirit that is calm."

Because delight gave way to grief, because primordial goodness was supplanted by nothing but evil and violence in the human heart, is it possible to do a restart? This too is a question that resounds throughout the biblical narrative. Is there a possibility for redemption, for new beginning? In place of this scarred face, weathered by all that it has seen and done, can't we start again with a fair one? In the face of the anxiety, fear, and shame that grips our hearts, is it possible to be graced with a spirit that is calm?

Not so quickly, replies the Holy One. In this covenantal argument the earth creature must take responsibility for the present calamity of cowardice and shame:

> "I never never turned aside," he said,
> "I never walked away.
> It was you who built the temple,
> It was you who covered up my face."

The story of the flood has already demonstrated that it isn't so easy just to start again. Like an addict released from rehab, given a second chance, the path of temptation is too strong for any quick solution. If there is a crisis here, if there is a breaking of covenant, then we need to look more closely at the roots. Here Cohen demonstrates a deeply prophetic vision of Israel's story. The Holy One, even the Holy One who sent them into exile and vacated the throne, never turned away. The Divine gaze was always lovingly upon the world born of love, was always on those called to covenant.

No, the father insists, "I never turned away/It was you who built the temple/it was you who covered up my face." Standing in the tradition of Jeremiah who has no use for those who repeat as a mantra, "The temple of the Lord, the temple of the Lord" (Jeremiah 7:4), this Jewish artist has the audacity to view the temple—that central symbol in the life of Israel, that site of the very presence of God, the very center of the cosmos—as a pagan departure from covenant. The temple, that establishment of so much of priestly Judaism, is dismissed as nothing less than an attempt to cover up the face of God.

So how does all of this help a soldier fighting for the very life of Israel in the Yom Kippur War? There is much debate about that. Cohen has tried to say that he was writing for soldiers on both sides, but that seems disingenuous.[22] Rather, I suggest that in the midst of this war, and in the midst of Cohen's own "war effort" as a performer for the troops, this song returns us to the heart of the covenantal relationship that is really at stake here. The song is a testimony to that covenantal dialogue, to the give and take in a covenantal relationship, and a call to return to faithfulness.

Twelve times the artist sings, "Yes and lover, lover, lover, lover, lover, lover, lover come back to me." And note that he repeats the word seven times. Perhaps these numbers are significant. Might the twelve represent the

22. Maltz, "Extraordinary Israeli Story."

twelve tribes of Israel, while the number seven harkens to the seven days of creation, the seventh being the number of completion, wholeness? Perhaps. But what is crucial is that this is a call from a lover to a lover. Come back to me. Come back to covenant. Come back to love. Come back home.

> And may the spirit of this song,
> May it rise up pure and free.
> May it be a shield for you,
> A shield against the enemy

May the spirit of this song with its evocative rehearsal of the heart of covenantal faith be a shield for you against the enemy, within and without. The enemy before you on the battlefield, but perhaps more profoundly, the enemy that leads you away from covenant. This is a song calling both listener and artist back to love, back to covenant. This is a song calling covenantal people to come back home, not to the structures and institutions of any religious or political systems, but to the Holy One himself.

HOMECOMING

From beginning to end, the biblical landscape is all about home. We could evocatively summarize the shape of this narrative as a story of home, home-breaking, home-making, and homecoming.[23] Not surprisingly, towards the end of his life, Cohen wrote a song precisely about such homecoming. "Going Home," on the 2012 *Old Ideas* album, is a song of a man reflecting on his life while preparing for his death. A man listening again to what his God might require of him. I hear this song in two voices. In the verses

23. Bouma-Prediger and Walsh, *Beyond Homelessness*, ch. 1.

we hear the voice of God reflecting on his servant Leonard. Or at least we hear God's servant Leonard musing on what it is that God might be saying to him at the end of his life. And in the chorus we hear the artist himself, letting go, relinquishing it all, prepared to go home.

> I love to speak with Leonard
> He's a sportsman and a shepherd
> He's a lazy bastard
> Living in a suit

The artist begins by taking the piss out of himself by having God make a joke at the artist's expense. Leonard Cohen is, of course, no sportsman. He might well be considered a shepherd. And he certainly lived much of his life in a suit. But a lazy bastard? Certainly not professionally. And certainly not spiritually, if we attend to the intensity of his spiritual quest. But maybe this laziness is akin to the idleness of his soul in "Born in Chains." Following Marcia Pally, might this be a judgment on Cohen's covenantal laziness?[24] Perhaps this is a confession that when it came to committed relationships, this artist really was a "lazy bastard." He didn't work hard enough at covenantal faithfulness. Maybe.

> But he does say what I tell him
> Even though it isn't welcome
> He just doesn't have the freedom
> To refuse
>
> He will speak these words of wisdom
> Like a sage, a man of vision
> Though he knows he's really nothing
> But the brief elaboration of a tube

---

24. Pally, *From This Broken Hill*, 74.

The poet who once sang, "I'm the little Jew who wrote the Bible,"[25] and who dared to take up the mantle of the prophet, here imagines God acknowledging that this lazy bastard did speak the words he was given. And with such words of wisdom he looked like a sage, a man of vision, even though he himself knew better. But the artist did have his own vision, his own self-understanding and sense of calling as a songwriter.

> He wants to write a love song
> An anthem of forgiving
> A manual for living
> with defeat
>
> A cry above the suffering
> A sacrifice recovering
> But that isn't what I need him
> To complete

That pretty much sums up what we love about Leonard, doesn't it? His body of work is a manual for living with defeat. That's why our defeated lives find comfort in his songs. His has been a cry above the suffering, which did not require numbness in relation to that suffering. And we sure as hell have needed anthems of forgiving, haven't we? That's great, replies God. But that's not what the Holy One needed him to complete. There is something more profound in store for this struggling and often tortured poet, now approaching the end of his life:

> I want him to be certain
> That he doesn't have a burden
> That he doesn't need a vision
> That he only has permission
> To do my instant bidding

---

25. "The Future."

> Which is to say what I have told him
> To repeat

Returning to our opening psalm from the *Book of Mercy* at the beginning of this chapter, the artist has had earnest strategies, he has been burdened to speak a word of truth, he has attempted to weave a vision through literature, song, and poetry, perhaps rewire some circuits wired wrong, and change a mind

> from slaughter
> in the name of peace,
> to honouring
> complexities[26]

And he's done all of this within a biblical landscape, shaped by a covenantal imagination. But as he prepares to go home, the Holy One wants to relieve him of such an artistic burden. Just listen. Just obey. To which the artist responds:

> Going home
> Without my sorrow
> Going home
> Sometime tomorrow
> Going home
> To where it's better
> Than before
>
> Going home
> Without my burden
> Going home
> Behind the curtain
> Going home
> Without this costume
> That I wore

---

26. "All my news," *Book of Longing*, 42.

God has offered to take away the poet's burden, and the poet accepts the offer. The poet who would raise a cry above the suffering and compose a manual for defeat is going home without his sorrow. Going home behind the curtain, into the holy of holies, into the presence of God, into the throne room. And this lazy bastard living in a suit, can finally take off the costume that he wore. Here is how an earlier poet of the covenant imagined such a homecoming:

Revelation 21:1-5

Then I saw "a new heaven and a new earth,"
for the first heaven and the first earth had passed
    away,
and there was no longer any sea.

I saw the Holy City, the new Jerusalem,
coming down out of heaven from God,
prepared as a bride beautifully dressed for her
    husband.
And I heard a loud voice from the throne saying,

"Look! God's dwelling place is now among the people,
and God will dwell with them.
They will be God's people, and God
will be with them and be their God.

Every tear will be wiped from their eyes.
There will be no more death,
or mourning or crying or pain,
for the old order of things has passed away."

The One who was seated on the throne said,
"I am making everything new!"

Then the Voice said,

> "Write this down, for these words are trustworthy and true."

And the Jewish poet from Montreal echoes the ancient Jewish poet John of Patmos by singing:

> Going home
> Without my sorrow
> Going home
> Sometime tomorrow
> Going home
> To where it's better
> Than before
>
> Going home
> Without my burden
> Going home
> Behind the curtain
> Going home
> Without this costume
> That I wore

The home created in love is recreated in forgiveness. The home of covenantal relationship eschews all costumes that hide the truth. The home called into being by a Voice that says let there be, is a home renewed by a voice that says, "Come." Come home to where it is better than before. Home restored.

CHAPTER 3

When they said "Repent," I wondered what they meant

Cohen and the Prophetic Voice

We began our theological investigation into the music, poetry, and prayers of Leonard Cohen by tracing the ubiquitous presence of Jesus in Cohen's songs. Wherever you look, from "Suzanne" on the first album to "It Seemed the Better Way" on the last album before Leonard's death in 2016, there is a conversation with Jesus. And then in the last chapter we broadened the scope of the conversation by tracing some of the song lines of what Cohen calls the biblical landscape of his work and we saw that "covenant" functions as a unifying and grounding theme in Cohen's poetic imagination. Engaging a number of Cohen's songs and poems, we traversed that landscape from creation to flood, from delight to grief, from the binding of Isaac to the exodus from Egypt, from the giving of the law to the covenantal dialogue of exile and return.

COVENANTAL HOMECOMING

It all comes together, I suggest, with the theme of home. If we are talking about covenant, then we are talking about home. Home is at the very heart of a biblical vision of life. Indeed, this is at the very heart of a biblical understanding of God and the cosmos. Since the whole story begins with the Holy One calling into being a creational home, full of generative love, it is no wonder that the promise of covenant is for a homeland. And it is not surprising that the Torah is a manual for homemaking or that the breaking of covenant necessarily results in the homelessness of exile. So, of course, the longing and hope in exile is always for homecoming, but, even while waiting for that return, the exilic community is still called to homemaking in the midst of exile.[1] Moreover, that incurable longing for home is sustained throughout the biblical narrative right to the vision at the end of the book of Revelation that imagines God making home on a renewed earth, dwelling with us as our God. It is all about home: homemaking, home-breaking, homelessness, and homecoming. If you are a child of the covenant, living within a biblical landscape, then your imagination has been shaped by this story of home, homelessness, and homecoming. In such an imagination it is crucial to understand that the longing for home with God isn't a spirituality of escape, but is a vision that gets to the very heart of life together with God in this good creational home. And even though Cohen is, like all of us, party to home-breaking and fleeing from covenant, it isn't surprising that at his best, he gives voice to a covenantal spirituality of home.

---

1. Jeremiah 29:4–7.

Again, we find deep and eloquent resources for such a spirituality in Cohen's *Book of Mercy*. Adapting the forty-first psalm of that collection, I offer another prayer litany that invites us to pray with Leonard towards a homecoming that heals the broken heart and binds us anew to covenantal homemaking.

Let us pray.

> I look far, I forget you, and I'm lost.
> I lift my hands to you.
> I kneel toward my heart.
>
> *I have no other home.*
> *My heart is here.*
>
> I end the day in mercy
> that I wasted in despair.
>
> *Bind me to you.*
> *I fall away.*
> *Bind me, ease of my heart,*
> *bind me to your love.*
>
> Gentle things you return to me,
> and duties that are sweet.
> And you say, I am in this heart,
> I and my name are here.
>
> *I have no other home.*
> *My heart is here.*
>
> Everywhere the blades turn,
> in every thought the butchery,
> and it is raw where I wander.
>
> *Bind me to you.*
> *I fall away.*

WHEN THEY SAID "REPENT," I WONDERED WHAT THEY MEANT

Bind me, ease of my heart,
bind me to your love.

You hide me in the shelter of your name,
and you open the hardness to tears.

I have no other home.
My heart is here.

The drifting is to you,
and the swell of suffering
breaks toward you.

Bind me to you.
I fall away.
Bind me, ease of my heart,
bind me to your love.

You draw me back to close my eyes,
to bless your name in speechlessness.

I have no other home.
My heart is here.

Blessed are you
in the smallness of your whispering.
Blessed are you who speaks
to the unworthy.

Bind me to you.
I fall away.
Bind me, ease of my heart,
bind me to your love.

There is no sentimentality of "home sweet home" in this prayer. And if there is any sense that "home is where the heart is," it is clear that this is a broken heart. This prayer gives voice to a homecoming of returning in the face of loss, a homecoming of remembering in the face of homeless amnesia. This is a homecoming to mercy in the face of despair, of gentleness in the face of savage butchery. In the ruins of severed and broken relationships, this is a homecoming of covenantal binding. Hardened homeless hearts find a shelter for their tears, and in the midst of debilitating suffering and shame, we meet a homecoming of gracious welcome. But the fact that this is a homecoming in the face of loss, amnesia, despair, butchery, brokenness, hardness of heart, suffering, and shame tells us that home is both the site of return and exile, healing and suffering, welcome and rejection, love and anger. Just ask Jesus.

JESUS GOES HOME

You see, there was quite the buzz in the Nazareth synagogue that Sabbath day. The homegrown lad who had been making a name for himself throughout the land with his wordsmithing was coming home to speak to the community. The thirty-year-old rabbi opened the Isaiah scroll and began to read the words of that ancient prophet.

> *Luke 4:18–19*
>
> The Spirit of the Lord is upon me,
> because he has anointed me
> to bring good news to the poor.
> He has sent me to proclaim release to captives
> and recovery of sight to the blind,
> to let the oppressed go free,
> to proclaim the year of the Lord's favor.

That was a crowd-pleaser. That was like singing one of the hits. And that was the kind of hope that kept folks going (and likely returning for the next show). Good news to the poor? That's us, in small-town Nazareth. Release to captives? Isn't that our life under the rule of the damn Romans? Let the oppressed go free? If we aren't the oppressed, then who is?

And then, well, then it gets even better! The Word of Words, Measure of all Measures, the Word that is at the heart of Torah, the Measure that equals all the scales, this hope of all hopes . . . proclaims the year of the Lord's favor! Here is a proclamation of the liberation that is at the heart of the Torah. This is proclaiming nothing less than the year of Jubilee, the year of redemption, the Sabbath of all Sabbaths, the promise of return. Here, in the midst of their continued exile in their own land, Jesus reads a passage that sings a song of radical homecoming!

Some in the audience might have noticed that he cut the Isaiah reading short. They might have noticed that this wordsmith stopped mid-sentence. They might have been mouthing the words to come from this song of Isaiah: ". . . to proclaim the year of the Lord's favor *and the day of vengeance of our God* . . ." because, Lord knows, they'd like to see some vengeance on their oppressors.[2] But if the rabbi wanted to stop with Jubilee good news, that was fine by them. And then, with anticipation rising in the community, with what could only be described as a hunger for the Word, the community waited with rapt attention as the hometown celebrity sat down to teach.

"Today this scripture is fulfilled in your hearing," he said. That's it. "Today this scripture is fulfilled in your hearing." Shortest sermon in history. And the crowd goes wild. The sense of hometown pride swelled, as this radical word of hope is delivered with prophetic authority. Everyone is happy, even the ones who were hoping for

2. Isaiah 61:2.

a little vengeance. But then Jesus turns it all on its head and deliberately provokes the community. Anticipating that they might want an encore, that they might be looking for a miracle or two, Jesus says, "No prophet is accepted in the prophet's hometown" (Luke 4:24), and then offers a couple of stories that were not in the preferred repertoire of bedtime tales for the children. These were never the hits in the community's favorite Bible stories. He references the stories of Elijah and Elisha, two legendary prophets who brought remarkable healing to pagans, not Hebrew covenant members. The point was clear. The local poet, who was the pride of the community and received with great applause, dropped the line about vengeance from his song because there would not be any vengeance. But, worse than that, the meaning of these two stories about Elijah and Elisha also made it clear that the good news to the poor and the release of captives could be granted to outsiders while the insiders were left out. And, proving the dictum that a prophet is never accepted in their hometown, the crowd's pride turned to rage, their welcome-home party became a murderous mob, and they were so consumed in their anger that they sought to throw Jesus off a cliff. Well, this story of Jesus bears some resemblance to another story.

LEONARD GOES HOME

There was quite the buzz in the Jewish Public Library for that evening lecture. The homegrown Montreal lad who had been making a name for himself throughout the land with his wordsmithing was coming home to speak to the community. A thirty-year-old local poet, celebrated throughout the land in the world of arts and letters, came to the library in 1964 to talk about an older Jewish poet, A. M. Klein, who was by then confined to a psychiatric hospital.

The lecture was called "Loneliness and History." But, unlike Jesus, Leonard Cohen picks a fight from the outset. This young and apparently brash poet dared to criticize the esteemed Klein for the predominance of the generic pronoun "we" over the personal pronoun "I." Cohen said:

> I remember A. M. Klein speaking, whose poems disturbed me because at certain moments in them he used the word "we" instead of the word "I," because he spoke with too much responsibility, he was too much a champion of the cause, too much the theorist of the Jewish party line.[3]

Klein's employment of "we" over "I," Cohen insisted, was indicative of him employing a priestly rather than a prophet voice as a poet in the Jewish community. Klein became the wordsmith of affluent Montreal Jewry, a representative of the community, speaking on behalf of the community, indeed, writing speeches for the elite of the community. "He became their clown," Cohen thundered. "He spoke to men who despised the activity he loved most. He raised money. He chose to be a priest and protect the dead ritual. And now we have his silence."[4] And this, Cohen provocatively argued, is a betrayal of the poet's prophetic calling. The prophet has the audacity to address the community with the pronoun "I." So the young Cohen, before the elite of Montreal Jewry, took on the mantle that his teacher had discarded and spoke with the arrogant abrasiveness of the first-person pronoun, daring to proclaim, "I believe

3. Cited by Leibovitz, *Broken Hallelujah*, 83.
4. Cited by Leibovitz, *Broken Hallelujah*, 84.

that the God worshipped in our synagogues is a hideous distortion of a supreme idea—and deserves to be attacked and destroyed. I consider it one of my duties to expose the platitude that we have created."[5]

Refusing to be gentle with his neighbors and fellow members of the synagogue, he argued that the community was marked by the fossils of the original energy, a fossilized version of an ancient faith, and that priests were invariably the keepers of such fossils, the museum curators of that ancient faith. The prophet is not interested in fossils or dead faith. The prophet has no use for a faith frozen in time. Rather, the prophet pursues the faith as it changes form, following it into regions of danger and threat. And thus, the prophet is invariably marginalized, pushed to the edge of the community, and left in the depths of loneliness in the midst of history.

Not surprisingly, the "fossils" didn't respond well to this brash and often foul-mouthed young poet fashioning himself as a prophet. The argument was hot and the audacity of this man was condemned. His self-appointed authority to speak to the community in such tones—not to mention his insult towards a revered member of the community, locked in an asylum and unable to defend himself—created an anger and sense of betrayal. There was a lot of shouting. Kind of like Jesus in Nazareth.

So another public meeting was set up for the next week, in which the young Cohen would answer his critics. A panel of leaders assembled, the room filled with community members, and Mr. Cohen simply didn't come back. Like Jesus, he walked through the crisis he had created and went away, leaving the mob behind. Jesus went throughout Galilee and Judea, and ultimately

---

5. Cited by Leibovitz, *Broken Hallelujah*, 85.

to Jerusalem to die. Leonard went to Hydra, then to New York, Nashville, back and forth to Montreal, up Mount Baldy, and ultimately to Los Angeles to die. They both knew that in a world of cover-up and self-justification there will always be conflict. And they both knew that to take on the mantle of a prophet is to see that conflict at the very heart of home.

THE PROPHET GOES TO WAR

If we were right in the last chapter arguing that for Cohen—and, indeed, within the biblical landscape itself—covenant goes all the way down and that covenant is the glue of all things, then I think we can suggest that where there is a breaking of covenant there will be conflict permeating all things. And Cohen seems to have been drawn to such conflict from an early age. A few years before his Montreal Jewish Public Library speech, Cohen wrote to his brother-in-law to explain his presence in the war zone of Cuba during the 1961 Bay of Pigs invasion. He placed the Cuba crisis in a larger and deeper context of war:

> It is the war between those who conceive of existence as a dynamic rainbow, and those who conceive of it as a grey monotone, between those who are willing to acknowledge the endless possibilities, agonies, delights, mysteries and destinies of the human predicament, and those who meet every human question with a rigid set of answers, some immutable inheritance from a father or a god or a revolution. This is the old war, Athens against Sparta, Socrates against Athens, Isaiah against the priests, the

> war that deeply involves our "western civilization," the one to which I am committed.[6]

There is a war, and it seems to go all the way down. While the priest might seek appeasement or denial, blithely intoning, "The temple of the Lord! The temple of the Lord!" (Jeremiah 7:4) or even "The synagogue! The church! The Canadian way of life!," the prophet breaks through numbness with passion and smashes the self-secure comfort of denial with pointed and abrasive speech. Cohen's "There is a War," released on the 1974 album, *New Skin for the Old Ceremony*, takes precisely such a prophetic voice.

> There is a war between the rich and poor
> A war between the man and the woman
> There is a war between the ones who say there is a war
> And the ones who say there isn't
> Why don't you come on back to the war, that's right, get in it
> Why don't you come on back to the war, it's just beginning

Writing in the wake of the Yom Kippur War in 1973, Cohen returned to themes that had been percolating for years. Let's name things as they are. There is a class war between the rich and poor, male and female, black and white, left and right. This is a war that takes on dimensions of economic inequity, gender discrimination, racism, and ideology. This is a war that permeates all of life, even the odds and the evens. And while the priest may seek to comfort us in the midst of the war (or even to assure us that the forces of God and the good are clearly on our side in this war), the prophet wants to name the war and to demand that we find our place.

---

6. Cited in Leibovitz, *Broken Hallelujah*, 101.

There is no escaping the conflict at the heart of things. There is no safe place to stand in a massacre. There are no innocent bystanders. There is a war, and the prophet calls us to take sides. There is a war, and no touristic voyeurism is allowed. As anxious and uncomfortable as this will make us, the prophet says that we must all be mobilized in the conflict at the heart of things. We need to take sides. The poet/prophet knows that such a call to engagement will not be popular.

> You cannot stand what I've become
> You much prefer the gentleman I was before
> I was so easy to defeat, I was so easy to control
> I didn't even know there was a war

Cohen acknowledges that not only is this an uncharitable song, it could also easily devolve into a slogan. Nonetheless, this is the kind of stance that is necessary if one lives in a biblical landscape, standing in the tradition of the prophetic voice. And that voice is, invariably, a voice of endings. Setting the song in a broader cultural context, the poet once explained: "Even in the midst of this flood, or catastrophe, which we are in, these are the days of the flood, these are the final days, in a sense all the institutions are, and have been swept away and the ethical question is, what is the proper behaviour, what is the appropriate behaviour in the midst of a catastrophe?"[7] This is, of course, prophetic language. And, akin to most prophetic language, such a view of the world comes across as the debilitating ramblings of a depressed personality. There is nothing immediately self-evident about such pronouncements and they are not easily received.

---

7. Rasky, dir., *Song of Leonard Cohen*.

ISAIAH

Of course, Cohen understood the place of the prophet and the counterintuitive nature of the prophetic word. Having spent much time studying Isaiah with his maternal grandfather, the talmudic scholar Solomon Klonitsky-Kline, Cohen knew that Isaiah's assessment of his times was radically out of step with the dominant consensus. In his 1961 collection of poems *The Spice-Box of Earth*, we find the poem "Isaiah," which begins with a description of the prosperity and security that characterized the reign of King Uzziah.[8]

> Between the mountains of spices
> the cities thrust up pearl domes and filigree spires.
> Never before was Jerusalem so beautiful.
>
> . . .
>
> Commerce like a strong wild garden
>   flourished in the street.
> The coins were bright, the crest on the coins precise,
> new ones looked almost wet.

So, why, the poet wonders, would an eloquent and well-educated man like Isaiah complain? If the shops are flush with rich spices, the cities are emerging in grandeur and beauty, the economy is strong and the coin minters can't keep up with the demand for more currency, then what is the problem?

> Why did Isaiah rage and cry,
> Jerusalem is ruined,
>   your cities are burned with fire?
> On the fragrant hills of Gilboa
> were the shepherds ever calmer,

---

8. Cohen, *Stranger Music*, 40–42.

> the sheep fatter, the white wool whiter?
> There were fig trees, cedars, orchards
> where men worked in perfume all day long.
> New mines as fresh as pomegranates.
> > Robbers were gone from the roads,
> > the highways were straight.
> There were years of wheat against famine . . .

It was a time of affluence, economic growth, and military security. Had things ever been better? So . . .

> Why then this fool Isaiah,
> smelling vaguely of wilderness himself,
> why did he shout,
> > Your city is desolate?
> . . .
>
> Now plunged in unutterable love
> Isaiah wanders, chosen, stumbling
> against the sculptured walls which consume
> their full age in his embrace and powder
> as he goes by. He reels beyond
> > the falling dust of spires and domes,
> obliterating ritual: the Holy Name, half-spoken,
> is lost on the cantor's tongue; their pages barren,
> congregations blink, agonized and dumb.

It is with unutterable love that Isaiah utters his prophecy. It is with unutterable love that this chosen one wanders, stumbling through Israel's communal history. And it is with unutterable love that the prophet comes with an alternative vision, an imagination that is just beyond the range of normal sight, a counter-testimony to the self-secure narrative of the regime.

RAGS OF LIGHT

Isaiah 2:5–18

O house of Jacob,
    come, let us walk
in the light of the Lord!

You have forsaken your people,
    the house of Jacob,
for they are full of diviners from the East
    and of soothsayers like the Philistines,
    and they clasp hands with foreigners.

Their land is filled with silver and gold,
    and there is no end to their treasures;
their land is filled with horses,
    and there is no end to their chariots.

Their land is filled with idols;
    they bow down to the work of their hands,
    to what their own fingers have made.

And so people are humbled,
    and everyone is brought low—
    do not forgive them!
Enter into the rock,
    and hide in the dust
from the terror of the Lord
    and from the glory of his majesty.

The haughty eyes of people shall be brought low,
    and the pride of everyone shall be humbled,
and the Lord alone will be exalted on that day.

For the Lord of hosts has a day
    against all that is proud and lofty,
    against all that is lifted up and high;
against all the cedars of Lebanon,
    lofty and lifted up;

> and against all the oaks of Bashan;
> against all the high mountains
> and against all the lofty hills;
> against every high tower
> and against every fortified wall;
> against all the ships of Tarshish
> and against all the highly prized vessels.
>
> The haughtiness of people shall be humbled,
> and the pride of everyone shall be brought low,
> and the Lord alone will be exalted on that day.
> The idols shall utterly pass away.

Be fruitful, multiply, and fill the earth was the mandate at the beginning of the story. And the prophet perceives a city that is full indeed. Full of the intellectual elite from various cultures, serving as consultants to the ruling authorities, all paid a handsome wage. The city is full of silver and gold and there is no end to their treasures. Wealth is being generated for the economic elite. Full of horses and chariots, the tools of a strong security establishment, the economic and political elite are well protected against external or internal threat. But this prophet sees more. He sees past the ideology of the ruling classes with their cosmopolitanism, endless treasures, and security apparatus, and he sees that this is a city full of idols. And that is the crucial moment in any prophetic vision. Any good cultural observer could see that Jerusalem was a world-class city of education, wealth, and security. It is the prophetic voice, however, that goes deeper and names the idolatry.

Within the context of covenant, then, once the diagnosis of idolatry has been discerned, the prognosis is grave. The prophet dares to imagine the impossible scenario of the whole system collapsing, with all of its wealth, power, and glory buried in the ruins. In a series of prophetic reversals the haughty eye is brought low, the proud and arrogant are humbled. In Isaiah's vision—which he shares with the whole prophetic tradition—the civilizational order of this city, built as it is on idolatry, will collapse and chaos will reign.

Why? Why can't such a clearly successful urban experiment succeed? Why must this city collapse? Why? Well, the contemporary Jewish prophet had it right. There is a war, and the Holy One is a combatant aligned *against* this city in all of its splendor, *against* this culture in all of its beauty, *against* this economy in all of its wealth, *against* this built environment in all of its arrogance. And contrary to everything that most would see looking at this city of idolatry, the prophet can see that "the idols shall utterly pass away." These idols that exude such power, permanence, and authority will utterly pass away. They will be so useless that when the collapse comes, when the arrogant and powerful are looking for a hole to crawl into, they'll have to throw away their idols to the moles and the bats. Empty-handed, they will leave these unclean symbols of cultural wealth for the pleasure of unclean animals. That's all that they will be good for.

EVERYBODY KNOWS

While shocking to most of his hearers, from Isaiah's perspective this is all self-evident. If your cultural life is rooted in idolatry, if covenantal amnesia breaks the bond with your God, if your life is formed by graven images and not conformed to the image of God, then it is a house built on sand and deceit, a house built on idolatry and oppression. From a prophetic perspective, this is stuff that everybody knows—especially Leonard Cohen. Released on the 1988 album *I'm Your Man,* here is the opening verse to Cohen's "Everybody Knows" (co-written with Sharon Robinson):

> Everybody knows that the dice are loaded
> Everybody rolls with their fingers crossed
> Everybody knows the war is over
> Everybody knows the good guys lost
> Everybody knows the fight was fixed
> The poor stay poor, the rich get rich
> That's how it goes
> Everybody knows

In contrast to a secular optimism in which history is getting better and better, progressing towards some kind of civilizational utopia, the prophet tells us that history is a crapshoot where the dice are loaded and the odds are against you. From geopolitics where the good guys—whoever they are—always lose, to the economic war of the rich against the poor, "progress" never means justice or equity. The game is fixed.

> Everybody knows that the boat is leaking
> Everybody knows that the captain lied
> Everybody got this broken feeling
> Like their father or their dog just died

This is a world of deceit, in which this leaky ship of fools that we call Western civilization is sinking, and the captains, the cultural leaders, the forces of normality are all liars. No wonder everybody's got this broken feeling; no wonder this sinking ship is mirrored by a sinking in the depths of our stomachs.

> Everybody knows that you love me baby
> Everybody knows that you really do
> Everybody knows that you've been faithful
> Ah, give or take a night or two

> Everybody knows you've been discreet
> But there were so many people you just had to meet
> Without your clothes

In a world of broken covenant, fidelity will always give way to sexual and spiritual promiscuity.

> Everybody knows the scene is dead
> But there's gonna be a meter on your bed
> That will disclose
> What everybody knows

No wonder "the scene is dead" and we've been reduced to the bare bones conflict of "it's me or you." This is the shape of cultural dissolution. And with almost prescient accuracy this late-/postmodern poet proclaims that "Everybody knows that the Plague is coming/Everybody knows that it's moving fast." Like the prophets before him, Cohen recognizes that in the breaking of covenant there is a creation-wide disharmony, manifest in both ecological destruction and plagues that threaten life at its very foundation.

> And everybody knows that you're in trouble
> Everybody knows what you've been through
> From the bloody cross on top of Calvary
> To the beach of Malibu
> Everybody knows it's coming apart
> Take one last look at this Sacred Heart
> Before it blows
> And everybody knows

The prophetic voice is seldom one of nuance. Prophets don't hedge their bets. They do not aspire towards a balanced perspective. Rather, their word is stark in its devastating abrasiveness. But this isn't anger for anger's sake. No, this is anger for grief's sake. And this grief, betrayal, and brokenness spans from the cross of Calvary to the beach at Malibu; from the suffering of Jesus to the decadence of a celebrity beach. Wherever you look, from the sacred to the profane, from the sublime to the ridiculous, it is all coming apart. But this isn't just a disaffected poet getting off on some dystopian vision. No, if this song is to stand in the tradition of the prophets, if this poet is to take up the mantle of Isaiah, then this dissolution of all things must reach the very heart of God. As we have seen, in a covenantal worldview if the world is broken, the Holy One is broken; if we are in a time of troubles, the Holy One is in trouble. You see,

> Everybody knows it's coming apart
> Take one last look at this Sacred Heart
> Before it blows
> And everybody knows

It wasn't just reading Isaiah with his grandfather that profoundly shaped the young Leonard Cohen. So also did the predominant Catholicism of the Montreal of his youth. And so it is the Sacred Heart of Jesus that is wounded anew, broken anew, left to bleed anew, in the blowing apart, the dissolution, the collapse and decline of Western civilization.

There is nothing smug about this prophetic evaluation of our situation. Indeed, while the tone of "Everybody Knows" is confident in its cultural appraisal, the foreboding nature of the song also gives it a feel of lament. And there is something foreboding and disquieting about this prophetic oracle of a song. You see, cultures, regimes, empires in decline are dangerous places. Sensing their mortality, fearing the inconceivable ending of the world as we know it, a dying culture will reach out to anything to preserve itself, to avoid death.

A PERIOD OF DANGER AND DECLINE

In a powerful prose piece called "Moving into a Period," published in the 2006 volume *Book of Longing*, Cohen prophetically anticipated much of what we are seeing today:

> We are moving into a period of bewilderment, a curious moment in which people find light in the midst of despair, and vertigo at the summit of their hopes. It is a religious moment also, and here is the danger. People will want to obey the voice of Authority, and many strange constructs of just what Authority is will arise in every mind. The family will appear again as the Foundation, much honoured, much praised, but those of us who have been pierced by other possibilities, we will merely go through the motions, albeit the motions of love. The public yearning for Order will invite stubborn uncompromising persons to impose it. The sadness of the zoo will fall upon society.[9]

The "religious moment" is at the heart of the human condition and at the center of hope. It is the site of ultimate authority in our lives. Therein is its danger. The kind of anomy, loss of direction, moral confusion, and anxiety that always accompanies a declining culture creates the conditions for precisely the kind of conservative entrenchment that we have seen in the last decade. A yearning for absolute Order, a fear of all that threatens that Order, together with a denial of alternative experience, all lead, within this kind of cultural milieu, to an absolutization of the heteronormative family, a fear of anything deemed

---

9. Cohen, "Moving into a Period," *Book of Longing*, 34.

"deviant," and the rise of an authoritarianism akin to the kind of neofascism that plagues Western culture today.

Such a sociocultural, religio-sexual regime breeds in a context of fear:

> You and I, who yearn for blameless intimacy, we will be unwilling to speak even the first words of inquisitive delight, for fear of reprisals. Everything desperate will live behind a joke. But I swear that I will stand within the range of your perfume.

While the poet sees the days of shame that are coming, he vows to stand with love and blameless intimacy, regardless of the severity of what is to come:

> How severe seems the moon tonight, like the face of an Iron Maiden, instead of the usual indistinct idiot.
>
> If you think Freud is dishonoured now, and Einstein, and Hemingway, just wait and see what is to be done with all the white hair, by those who come after me.

Not only will there be a dismissal of the progressive voices of the past, there will be book burning, rewriting of the educational curricula, and persecution. And like the moon darkened on Good Friday, so the benign symbolic appearance of the moon will be transformed into a legendary symbol of torture.

But the poet does not leave us there. The prophet brings a word of warning, a word of judgment, a word that cuts through the idolatry of the present, but never without hope. And so Cohen moves from one symbol of torture to another:

> But there will be a Cross, a sign, that some will understand; a secret meeting, a warning, a Jerusalem hidden in Jerusalem. I will be wearing white clothes, as usual, and I will enter The Innermost Place as I have done generation upon generation, to entreat, to plead, to justify. I will enter the chamber of the Bride and the Bridegroom, and no one will follow me.
>
> Have no doubt, in the near future we will be seeing and hearing much more of this sort of thing from people like myself.

While hope for a remnant in which the covenant is sustained and renewed in a secret community, even in the face of dissolution, is common amongst the prophets, Cohen's appeal to the cross remains unique and shocking. The very symbol that has been used as a weapon against Jews and infidels throughout history, the very symbol that was carried to the Capitol on January 6, 2021, the very symbol of the colonialism that is now in decline—*that very symbol!*—springs forth in this poet's prophetic vision of hope after the deluge. But perhaps the cross can resonate so deeply with someone so attuned to Isaiah, someone who knows that a suffering servant is key to this prophet's vision of the redemption of Israel.

And the symbolism returns to Jerusalem. The very Jerusalem that both Isaiah, and his disciple, Leonard, see collapse. This is a Jerusalem that Cohen describes as:

> Jerusalem of blood
> Jerusalem of amnesia
> Jerusalem of idolatry
> Jerusalem of Washington
> Jerusalem of Moscow
> Let the nations rejoice

Jerusalem has been destroyed[10]

In the face of that Jerusalem, the poet evokes a Jerusalem hidden in Jerusalem. A Jerusalem that lives up to its name as a City of Peace. That ancient symbol of Jerusalem as a site of redemption and the restoration of covenant. It is in that Jerusalem, that secret place, that our poet takes on not just the prophetic mantle, but also that of priest. But not yet.

GLADNESS IS BANISHED FROM THE EARTH

Given the affinity that Leonard Cohen has for the prophet Isaiah, the way in which this artist can plumb the depths of depression and sorrow is not surprising. To catch the resonances between these two prophets in more depth, consider this oracle of utter cultural, civilizational, and ecological collapse.

Isaiah 24

> Now the Lord is about to lay waste the earth and make it desolate,
>   and he will twist its surface and scatter its inhabitants.
> And it shall be, as with the people, so with the priest;
>   as with the male slave, so with his master;
>   as with the female slave, so with her mistress;
> as with the buyer, so with the seller;
>   as with the lender, so with the borrower;
>   as with the creditor, so with the debtor.
> The earth shall be utterly laid waste and utterly despoiled,
>   for the Lord has spoken this word. (1–3)

---

10. Cohen, *Book of Mercy*, #25.

In the "Tower of Song" (from the 1988 album *I'm Your Man*), Cohen sang, "Now, you can say that I've grown bitter but of this you may be sure/The rich have got their channels in the bedrooms of the poor/And there's a mighty judgement coming, but I may be wrong."[11] Isaiah, however, has no second thoughts about his word of judgment. He doesn't ever seem to countenance that he may be wrong. The evidence against us is too great. There is a mighty judgment coming, says the prophet, and it is a mighty leveler. No one escapes in this prophetic vision, certainly not the elite. And, given his own covenantal understanding of the world, Isaiah doesn't shrink from declaring the cosmic, indeed ecological, scope of this judgment.

> The earth dries up and withers;
>   the world languishes and withers;
>   the heavens languish together with the earth.
> The earth lies polluted
>   under its inhabitants,
> for they have transgressed laws,
>   violated the statutes,
>   broken the everlasting covenant.
> Therefore a curse devours the earth,
>   and its inhabitants suffer for their guilt;
> therefore the inhabitants of the earth dwindled,
>   and few people are left. (4–6)

Again, because covenant is the heart of all creation, any breaking of covenant and disregard of the measure of all measures that is the Torah, results in a guilt and a curse that rushes through all of creation like a tsunami. If Torah is the word of life, if the covenant offers a choice between

---

11. Cohen, *Stranger Music*, 363.

blessing and curse, life and death, then the breaking of covenant can only result in devastation.[12]

> The wine dries up;
>> the vine languishes;
>> all the merry-hearted sigh.
> The mirth of the timbrels is stilled;
>> the noise of the jubilant has ceased;
>> the mirth of the lyre is stilled.
> No longer do they drink wine with singing;
>> strong drink is bitter to those who drink it. (7–9)

The cacophony of cultural celebration, the joyful sound of music and partying is all rendered silent. It is a deadly silence. And you can't get a drink for love nor money.

> The city of chaos is broken down;
>> every house is shut up so that no one can enter. (10)

The City of Peace, the urban site of civilizational order is reduced to chaos, while homes are shut up in self-protection, and hospitality drowns in an ocean of fear. No wonder,

> There is an outcry in the streets for lack of wine;
>> all joy has reached its eventide;
>> the gladness of the earth is banished. (11)

And so, lacking even a cheap wine to drown our sorrows, we come to one of the most devastating verses in the whole Bible. Perhaps second only to what we have heard from Genesis 6:6 that the Lord God "was sorry" for creating humankind, Isaiah here reflects the wild regret of the Creator in the sorrow of the creation. All joy has reached its eventide. The sun has gone down on joy, not to rise again.

12. Deuteronomy 30:15–20.

Does it get more devastating than that? The gladness of the earth, the giddy delight that permeated creation at its birth, the mutual joy of Creator and creature in an ecstatic dance of bringing forth, has been banished from the earth. Joy has been sent into exile. And so, if there is no gladness left on the earth, if joy has reached its eventide, then what is left?

> Desolation is left in the city;
> the gates are battered into ruins. (12)

The gates offer neither protection nor welcome. The market stalls are empty. There are no musicians. The judgments of the wise are not being rendered in the gates. And so the prophet concludes:

> The earth is utterly broken;
> the earth is torn apart;
> the earth is violently shaken.
> The earth staggers like a drunkard;
> it sways like a hut;
> its transgression lies heavy upon it,
> and it falls and will not rise again. (19–20)

Utterly broken. Torn apart. Violently shaken. It falls and will not rise again.

In the darkness of that broken night, that eventide of joy and impending chaos, Isaiah's late-/postmodern disciple released an oracle called "The Future" on the 1992 album of the same name.[13]

> Give me back my broken night
> My mirrored room, my secret life
> It's lonely here
> There's no one left to torture
> Give me absolute control

13. Cohen, *Stranger Music*, 370–72.

Over every living soul
And lie beside me, baby
That's an order

Give me crack and anal sex
Take the only tree that's left
And stuff it up the hole
In your culture
Give me back the Berlin wall
Give me Stalin and St. Paul
I've seen the future, brother
It is murder

With a killer dance beat and little ambiguity, the poet unambiguously takes on the mantle of the prophet. Typically out of step with the pundits of normality, this oracle has its origin in a minority report on the unfolding of history. While many cultural analysts in the West greeted the fall of the Berlin Wall as ushering in a new era of peace in the wonderful march of civilizational progress, Cohen had a different take on things. In a 1993 interview on MTV he said:

> "When the Berlin Wall came down, which is what occasioned most of the songs on [*The Future*], everyone was rejoicing. Well of course I'm expected to be dismal and gloomy about these matters, but I thought it's a wonderful thing the wall's coming down but a lot of suffering is going to unfold also because of this wall coming down. So I say in the song: 'Give me back the Berlin Wall, give me Stalin and St. Paul, I've seen the future, brothers, it is murder.' I said, you know, you're gonna be happy with Stalin and the wall and your little hole in the ozone layer that you can't repair. These things are gonna sound like the Golden Age compared

to what's coming down—and it's starting to come down. The excrement is about to hit the ventilator."[14] As early as 1989, Cohen countered the optimism of the impending dissolution of the Soviet Union. "You're going to settle for the Berlin Wall when you see what's coming next. You're going to settle for a hole in the ozone layer. You'll settle for crack. You'll settle for social unrest. You'll settle for the L.A. Riots. This is kindergarten stuff compared with the homicidal impulse that is developing in every breast."[15]

In the shadow of a world historical event, a changing of epochs, Cohen does not shrink from his prophetic calling. Indeed, we could almost read "The Future" as Cohen's prophetic coming out party. By singing, "You don't know me from the wind/You never will, you never did/I'm the little Jew/who wrote the Bible," Cohen unapologetically stands in the prophetic tradition of deep critique and a cultural discernment that goes to the spiritual heart of the crises before us. Like Isaiah and Jeremiah, like Ezekiel and Amos, "I've seen the nations rise and fall/I've heard their stories, heard them all." And, like those prophets before him, he is a prophet of ending: "Your servant here, he has been told/to say it clear, to say it cold:/it's over it ain't going any further." "The Future" is an oracle of cultural collapse. And echoing Ezekiel 10, our postmodern prophet sings, "And now the wheels of heaven stop/you feel the devil's riding crop/get ready for the future/it is murder." When the wheels of heaven stop that is an indication that the Holy One has abandoned

14. 1993 MTV interview, https://www.youtube.com/watch?v=IgTVomEoiWU&t=479s

15. Quoted by Raab, "Cohen's Biblical Vision."

us to a period of dissolution, in which all distinctions dissolve and we are left sliding in all directions.

> Things are going to slide
> Slide in all directions
> Won't be nothing (won't be)
> Nothing you can measure anymore
> The blizzard, the blizzard of the world
> Has crossed the threshold
> And it's overturned
> The order of the soul

I hear this as a clear reference to Friedrich Nietzsche's "Parable of the Madman."

> Where are we headed? Are we not endlessly plunging—backwards, sideways, forwards, in all directions? Is there an up and a down anymore? Do we not wander as if through an endless nothingness? Do we not feel the breath of empty space? Hasn't it grown colder?[16]

This isn't a slippery slope, sliding in a particular direction. No this is the kind of out-of-control slide of a car in a blizzard, with no point of orientation and absolutely no control. And that, the prophet proclaims, is more terrifying than the false absolutes of the past. So give me back absolute control, and lie beside me baby, that's an order. So "give me back the Berlin Wall/give me Stalin and St. Paul/give me Christ/or give me Hiroshima." Give me anything that I can hold onto because anything is better than the nothing that we are left with at the end of civilization. This blizzard of the world is no longer "out there." No, it has crossed the threshold and invaded our homes. This blizzard of the world is no longer a storm brewing off in

---

16. In Nietzsche, *Gay Science,* par. 125.

the distance, it has crossed the threshold, gone past the point of no return. And everything is up for grabs.

"There'll be the breaking/of the ancient western code/your private life will suddenly explode." Whatever "ancient western code" gave coherence to our lives, whatever allowed us to hold together some semblance of a private life, has now been irreparably broken. Whatever gave us some secure sense of identity, some sense of our own, independent egos, whatever order of the soul we might have assumed, has been violently overturned. And the result is chaos, shame, terror, humiliation, desecration, and murder. "There will be phantoms/there'll be fires on the road/and the white man dancing." Civilization devolves into a paranoid tribalism, superstition, suspicion, and violence. Gary Shapiro summarizes this song well: "Dehumanization, environmental disaster, loss of individuality and privacy, terror and humiliation are what the future has in store. Cohen's future gives a voice to our fears." He concludes, "In 'The Future' there no longer is a future. It is a future robbed of futurity, of any sense of open possibility."[17] "It's over, it ain't going any further."

Does any of this sound familiar? Is this resonating with anything that we have seen in the last number of years in the United States and throughout Western culture? This is a chaotic scene of the end of things in which joy has reached its eventide. The world languishes and withers. The mirth of the timbrels gives way to the lousy little poets. The noise of the jubilant has ceased. Things slide in every direction in this broken-down culture of chaos. And the earth, together with all of humanity's

---

17. Gary Shapiro, "End of the World and Other Times in 'The Future,'" in Holt, ed., *Cohen and Philosophy*, 41.

cultural accomplishments, begins to violently shake. Cohen is channeling Isaiah for our times.

So what is a prophet to do? Well, what did Ezekiel say? "Thus says the Lord God: Repent and turn away from your idols; and turn away your faces from all your abomination" (Ezekiel 14:6). And, "Repent and turn away from your transgressions, otherwise iniquity will be your ruin" (Ezekiel 18:30). How about Isaiah? Does he have any promise in this catastrophe? Only in repentance. "Zion shall be redeemed by justice, and those in her who repent, by righteousness" (Isaiah 1:27). And what would Jesus do? Here is how the Gospel of Mark tells the story. "Jesus came to Galilee, proclaiming the good news of God, and saying, 'The time is fulfilled, and the kingdom of God is at hand; repent, and believe in the good news'" (Mark 1:14–15). To which the late modern prophet replies, "When they said, 'Repent,' I wondered what they meant." Twelve times in the chorus of "The Future," the word "repent" is repeated. And twelve times, the response is a total lack of understanding. It isn't as if the prophetic voice calls for repentance and the response is a self-justification. It isn't as if the prophetic voice says that we have been found not to measure up to some sort of clear moral standard and we appeal the verdict. No, the very notion of repentance, the very notion that our lives are subject to a moral judgment, a moral measurement, is itself unintelligible, lacking any meaning in a world that is sliding in all directions and there is nothing you can measure anymore. And so, with the "Word of Words/And Measure of all Measures," written "with burning letters" on his heart,[18] the prophet from Montreal lays bare our cultural condition in one of the most prophetically powerful songs of the last half-century.

18. Cohen, "Born in Chains," *Popular Problems*.

Does Cohen leave us lost in a dejected hopelessness? Not quite. Right in the middle of "The Future" there is a moment of profound hope. Right after the line, "I've seen the nations rise and fall/I've heard their stories, heard them all," Cohen sings, "but love's the only engine of survival." If love permeates the landscape of biblical faith, if love is the very foundation of creation, if love is the heart of covenant, and therefore the only path to full flourishing of life, then without love there is murder. Without love there is total collapse. "But love's the only engine of survival." That is the moment of hope in "The Future." And while "The Future" is the opening track on the vinyl album by the same name, the flip side of the album begins with "Democracy." We could say that this song, with its hard-won hope, functions as the flip side to the devastating vision of "The Future."

LOVE AND THE HOPE OF DEMOCRACY

If the self-congratulations of the West when the Berlin Wall fell and the Soviet Union collapsed was a hearty pat on the back of our democratic institutions, then Cohen's song "Democracy" functions as a cautionary, yet still hopeful, commentary. Written both as a check on the optimism of a Western conviction that democracy was about to blossom in the post-Soviet Bloc East, and yet also as a critique of the arrogant American claim that the USA is already a manifestation of democracy, Cohen's "Democracy" is a word of hope in the face of despair. In a 1993 interview about this song, Cohen said:

> Democracy is the great religion of the West. Probably the greatest religion because it affirms other religions; probably the greatest culture

> because it affirms other cultures. But it's based on faith, it's based on appetite for fraternity, it's based on love, and therefore it shares the characteristics of a religious movement. It's also like a religion in that it's never really been tried.[19]

That is quite an elevated vision of democracy, and I'm not totally sure that I share it. But if we take seriously the particular way in which Cohen discerns democracy as "coming to the USA," but not presently manifest there, and give credence to his claim that democracy is most deeply based in love—the very love that is the engine of survival—then this song continues to speak powerfully into our sociopolitical reality, some thirty years after its composition.

Because he died on the eve of the election of Donald Trump as the president of the United States, Cohen was saved from seeing the further dissolution of precisely the democracy that he so longed for. But it is in the shadow of that momentous event and in the darkness of what has become of America in the intervening years that Cohen's "Democracy" continues to speak with such prophetic power.

> It's coming through a hole in the air,
> from those nights in Tiananmen Square.
> It's coming from the feel
> that this ain't exactly real,
> or it's real, but it ain't exactly there.
>
> From the wars against disorder,
> from the sirens night and day,
> from the fires of the homeless,
> from the ashes of the gay:

19. Interview with Alberto Manzano, in Burger, ed., *Cohen on Cohen*, 320.

Democracy is coming to the U.S.A.

From the student protests for democracy in China when the song was written, or in Hong Kong today, to a disquieted sense of displacement at home, the poet discerns that something is afoot. It comes out of the chaos, with the sirens of emergency, amongst the dispossessed, the shamed, and the discarded. Democracy, sings Cohen, is coming to the USA. The biting irony was, of course, clear. Democracy is coming out of the most unlikely places to a country that assumes itself to be the epitome of the idea.

Do you know the difference between a one party state and a two party state? One. And that isn't very much. That is not much of a democracy. So how would democracy actually come to the USA? Or, for that matter, how would a true democracy come anywhere? Cohen answers in the chorus:

> Sail on, sail on
> O mighty Ship of State!
> To the Shores of Need
> Past the Reefs of Greed
> Through the Squalls of Hate
> Sail on, sail on, sail on, sail on.

Democracy must sail towards the shores of need. But you can't get to the shores of need without navigating *past* the reefs of greed and *through* the squalls of hate. Greed and hate are the constant temptations on the journey of democracy. They are the constant obstacles on the path to a truly civic society. Cohen says that we need to take this ship of state, with its cultural, political, and economic systems, toward the shores of need. We need to navigate precisely to those places of deep pain and hunger, oppression and disappointment, injustice and dismissal if there can ever be a true democracy. But greed and hate will always leave us shipwrecked. Greed and hate will always murder democracy and sabotage justice.

The US election on November 8, 2016 was an exercise in flawed democracy. Not just flawed because of the limitation of choice, or flawed because it was an exercise in plutocracy, or even flawed by the age-old practices of voter suppression. No, it was more deeply flawed than all of that. That election, and the political disaster that has plagued the United States ever since, was tragically flawed by greed and hate. A man whose whole life screams greed tapped into the real needs of millions of people by means of hate. The election of Donald Trump and the emergence of the Make America Great Again movement has taken this particular ship of state directly into the reefs of greed, sailing in the squalls of hate. And, like they always do, those reefs and squalls are causing a shipwreck.

Later in the song Cohen sings, "It's coming from the sorrow in the street/the holy places where the races meet." If there is to be any sense of renewed democracy in the USA it will be born on the streets of Black Lives Matter protests, in the homeless camps throughout the nation, in the movements for climate, LGBTQ+, and Native American justice. These are the holy places in America today. And Donald Trump has desecrated those holy places, as he desecrates and defiles everything he touches, including the highest office and the highest courts in the land. When Cohen sings (perhaps tongue in cheek), "Its coming to America first/the cradle of the best and the worst," we can only imagine that our prophet would have seen the rise of Trumpism as capitalizing on the worst.

If love is "the only engine of survival," then it is no wonder that Cohen sings, "the heart has got to open/in a fundamental way." Only in such an opening can there be any hope for a path beyond the present divisions, deceit, and fascism that we see threatening the future of the American experiment. I confess that I'm not that hopeful for democracy in the USA. Even if Trump were never reelected I fear that the American project will not survive without a level of mutual love that we have never seen in American culture. And it is clear that mutual love of country together with some sense of shared patriotism is too shallow and too empty—indeed, too idolatrous—a love to be the engine of any kind of survival. No, if there is to be love it will need to be deeper and higher than the state, and more profound than any ideology.

Cohen is right, the heart has got to open in a fundamental way. But what if that heart is so full of violence, so vile and angry, so closed in on itself, that there can be no opening? And Cohen is also right in perceiving that any such opening, any such vision and practice of human equality and justice will undoubtedly come from unexpected places. Don't look to the Supreme Court, but pay attention to "the fires of the homeless." Don't look to Focus on the Family, but bear witness to the "ashes of the gay." Don't look to the self-congratulatory elite, but join in solidarity with the "sorrow in the street." Don't look to the successful, but attend to "the wells of disappointment where/the women kneel to pray." Don't look to the captains of industry, but stand on the picket line with the brave, the bold, the battered hearts of workers trying to save their jobs and their futures. Don't look to the white nationalist piety of Make America Great Again, but search "for the grace of God in the desert here/and the desert far away." And don't look to the Congress, or the Constitution, or the White House, but dwell in the "staggering account of the Sermon on the Mount" which we "don't pretend to understand at all."

One of the things about reading the prophets is that their vision is so profound, indeed, so clear, precisely because they are always coming at things from different angles, different perspectives. When you are reading someone like Isaiah, you can get dizzy as he moves, sometimes within a sentence or two, from devastating critique to liberating hope, and back again, and back again, and back again. Employing wildly divergent metaphors we move from a grieved lover to an angry cultural critic, from a vineyard to a city of chaos, to a dimly burning wick, to children carried home in their nurses' arms.[20] We meet a sovereign Creator of all things, the Great I Am who calls people to covenant, and a Suffering Servant with no form or majesty and acquainted with grief.[21] So it is not surprising that the prophetic Leonard Cohen traverses many metaphors, and offers multiple visions to get a prophetic angle on things in our time. From the direct aim at the culture industries of fashion and music in "First We Take Manhattan" (*I'm Your Man*, 1988), to the extended meditation on our continued exile in Babylon of "By the Rivers Dark" (*Ten New Songs*, 2001), to the exhausted end-of-the-age party of "Closing Time" (*The Future*, 1992), Cohen has exercised his prophetic calling.

HOPE IN THE RUINS

Throughout my life—as a person who came of age at the end of something, who has been preoccupied with the interface of biblical faith and cultural dynamics, as a

---

20. Isaiah 1:2–9; 2:5–22; 5:1–7; 24:1–20; 42:1–9; 60:1–22.
21. Isaiah 42:5–9; 53:1–5.

teacher, and most importantly, as a pastor—it seems that I have been navigating my own life and helping young adults to navigate their lives through a landscape of ruins. If "Democracy" called us to navigate our lives "To the Shores of Need/Past the Reefs of Greed/Through the Squalls of Hate," then, almost a quarter of a century later, "Steer Your Way"(*You Want it Darker,* 2016) sharpens our navigational coordinates and calls us to a spiritual discipline of hope and, yes, repentance.

> Steer your way past the ruins
> Of the Altar and the Mall
> Steer your way through the fables
> Of creation and the fall
> Steer your way past the palaces
> That rise above the rot

How many of my students over the years have been steering their way past the ruins of the Altar and the Mall? How many have seen the dissolution of their faith in God parallel their spiritual exhaustion with the consumerism that has been the secular faith driving the modern world? In this period of cultural decline it seems that everything is up for grabs. But note that while the prophet counsels us to steer our way *past* the ruins of the Altar and the Mall, and even *past* the palaces of the 1 percent built upon the rot and the oppression of the majority of the world, he doesn't direct us to steer our way *past* the fables of creation and the fall, but *through* them. Indeed, it may well be that without these fables, without some sort of mythopoetic grounding that tells us where we are and what's wrong, there might be no way to navigate past the ruins in which we live.

This steering of our lives, this spiritual navigation, is a discipline that is always needed:

> Year by year
> Month by month
> Day by day
> Thought by thought

And like all spiritual disciplines, especially in moments of prophetic endings, in all closing times, there is some relinquishment necessary. If you are going to steer your way in such a context, then there is some baggage that will need to discarded.

> Steer your heart past the Truth
> You believed in yesterday
> Such as Fundamental Goodness
> And the Wisdom of the Way

Radical endings are deeply unsettling, and in such times of disorientation there may be some settled convictions, some final truths that can no longer stand the light of day. Maybe we need to rethink naive notions like fundamental goodness, or even various traditions of wisdom of the way. And it would seem telling that, at the end of his life, Cohen also sings, "Steer your heart, precious heart/ Past the women whom you bought." This too must be relinquished. Perhaps this heart has been too precious, too self-possessed in all of the relationships that it has consumed.

Steer past all of this, counsels our elderly prophet. Let it all go, because none of this will help you find your way, and none of it helped the prophet find his way. But again, there are some things that you need to steer *through*, not *past*.

> Steer your way through the pain
> That is far more real than you
> That smashed the Cosmic Model
> That blinded every View

> And please don't make me go there
> Tho' there be a God or not

The way forward is not by steering *past* the pain, but *through* it. In the prophetic imagination the reality of pain functions as counter-testimony to the status quo. The embrace of pathos breaks through numbness as it smashes Cosmic Models of the world that have rendered us blind. You see, steering our path *through* the pain, grief, and trauma, as uncomfortable as such a path may be, is the only way that we will regain our sight, the only way that we can have clarity of vision for the path ahead. It is true that steering our way through such pain will give us a vision through tear-filled eyes, but that is to be preferred to the blindness of the Cosmic Models that are being smashed all around us.

Musically, the bridge moves us along our path, almost giving us a bit of a dance step, a moment of choreography on the journey.

> They whisper still, the ancient stones
> The blunted mountains weep
> As he died to make men holy
> Let us die to make things cheap
> And say the Mea Culpa which you've probably forgot

Hidden in the irony of these lines we hear both a call to repentance, and a witness yet again that humankind is not in this mess alone. As we are trying to navigate our path through this period of civilizational, political, economic, ecological, and cultural ending, as we are groaning in travail longing for birth in the face of death, the artist tells us that all of creation groans with us. If the Cosmic Models of our own construction have rendered us blind, then the rest of creation invites us to listen more deeply. Listen, the poet admonishes us. Listen, people of the

Word. Listen "Shema Israel." And listen closely because it is just a whisper. "They whisper still, the ancient stones." The broken stones on which the Torah was written, the testimony stones bearing witness to covenantal promises, the boundary stones of covenantal inheritance, the stones on the side of the road that would cry "Hosanna" if the crowds were silenced.[22] They whisper still, these stones, as do all stones within a biblical landscape, all stones within a creation called and held in covenant. And in listening to that whisper, the stones will point us on our way. Those stones whisper, even while the blunted mountains weep. Echoing the prophecy to the mountains of Ezekiel 36, the contemporary prophet calls us to hear that weeping, hear the groaning and travail of mountains, subject to our exploitation, extraction, and desecration.

While Jesus died to make us holy, we die to make things cheap. We just die for the cheapest deal, and we are prepared to kill to get it. But what is it that the stones are whispering? What is the imperative entailed in the weeping of the mountains? One word. *Repent*. But this time we can't cop out and wonder what they meant. This time we cannot hide behind some vague notion of things sliding in all directions. The mountains and the stones are clear. All of creation is bearing witness against us. Things aren't sliding in all directions. They are sliding in one direction. They are sliding to destruction. They are sliding to judgment. So the prophet tells us that it is time to say the *mea culpa*, the first words in the prayer of confession, which we have conveniently forgotten. It is time to go to confession. Because without repentance, confession, and forgiveness, there is no way forward.

---

22. Exodus 31:18; Joshua 24:26–28; Deuteronomy 19:14; Luke 19:39–40.

Finally, our prophet counsels:

> Steer your way, O my heart
> Tho' I have no right to ask
> To the one who was never
> Never equal to the task
> Who knows he's been convicted
> Who knows he will be shot

Steer your way, recognizing that you are not equal to the task. Steer your way, knowing that this is a ship that has been sailing into the reefs of greed and powered by the squalls of hate. Steer your way, even though this ship is sinking and the captain lied. Steer your way, confessing that this is a mess of our own making, this is a breaking of covenant for which there is a just judgment.

That's where the prophet leaves us, before returning to the bridge one more time. "They whisper still, the ancient stones," and we are left straining to hear. But we can't. The prophet has unsettled our lives, ripped off our blinders, named the time we are in for the ending that it is, and unveiled our complicity—indeed, our sin. And the temptation is to be paralyzed in our guilt and our fear. The prophet has done his work, and now we need a priest. We need Leonard Cohen to live up to his priestly name. We need a greeting from the other side of sorrow and despair. We need to know that the pardon is in the mail.

CHAPTER 4

If it be your will
Cohen and the Priestly Calling

It is fair to say that Judy Collins was the first to seriously recognize Leonard Cohen as a great songwriter. It was Collins who first covered "Suzanne," bringing attention to the poetic vision, bare musical stylings, and intellectual depth of Cohen's work. It was Collins who first pushed Cohen onto a stage to perform (haltingly) his own song and who then needed to come back and perform the song with the artist after he had abandoned the microphone out of a spasm of anxiety. And so it is not surprising that it is Judy Collins who most succinctly summarized Cohen's work as "songs for the spirit when our spirits were strained to the breaking point."[1]

FROM THE BLUES TO FORGIVENESS

As we have seen, the phrase "spirits strained to their breaking point" captures well the spiritual ethos of both

1. Cited by Rose, "BEST."

Leonard Cohen and the prophetic tradition. Meeting us at our breaking point, this kind of poetry, song, and literature can tear us apart. And, as we have seen in the last chapter, when you begin to hear the resonance between Cohen and a biblical author like Isaiah, things can get pretty heavy. But if we are to move toward hope, then it cannot be cheap. From the beginning, Cohen has resisted any easy resolution and quick comfort in the security of the tradition. So, if we are to move from the prophetic to the priestly, from the *mea culpa* to forgiveness, then we can only do so with the prophetic voice still ringing in our ears.

Consider the devastating depiction of our cultural reality in "Almost Like the Blues," from the 2014 *Popular Problems* album. In this song the artist begins in the prophetic voice and offers only a hint of a priestly path forward towards the end of the song. The opening lines set the tone for the devastation to come: "I saw some people starving/there was murder, there was rape/the villages were burning/they were trying to escape." How do we respond to such a vision of horror? Well, most of us avert our gaze. We look the other way. "I couldn't meet their glances/I was staring at my shoes/It was acid, it was tragic/It was almost like the blues." How do you look such victims in the eye? How do you have the spiritual courage and emotional fortitude to face such tragedy, to be burned by such an acid? But there is also a death in such an averted gaze. "I have to die a little/Between each murderous plot/And when I'm finished thinking/I have to die a lot." There is a price to pay for our indifference. "Though I let my heart get frozen/To keep away the rot/My father says I'm chosen/My mother says I'm not." In the face of the death and decomposition of both our culture and our own souls, Cohen evokes the image of freezing our hearts to keep away the rot. But with a frozen heart, who are you? Living with a frozen heart and an averted gaze creates a crisis of identity. Within the biblical landscape of covenant, can the poet/prophet dare to imagine himself as "chosen"? Having so broken the covenant call to justice, can he continue to find his identity in that covenant? Having turned his back on love, is it possible to experience himself as beloved? Given his guilt, and given our collective guilt, having turned our back on love, dare we imagine new life in forgiveness?

The poet asks the experts and consults a tenured academic. "'There is no God in heaven/There is no hell below'/So says the great professor/Of all there is to know." So proclaims the arrogant atheism of modernity. The ancient mythology of God, and heaven and hell, has died at the hands of science, and is dismissed by the tenured purveyors of all knowledge. The poet, however, isn't so sure. In the face of the devastating blues of our time, in the face of the stench of our culture, and the violence of our own hearts, Cohen replies, "But I've had the invitation/That a sinner can't refuse/It's almost like salvation/It's almost like the blues."

How decidedly post-secular. How profoundly humble. In the face of a self-justifying atheism that can never deal with the depths of human brokenness, in the face of a naiveté in relation to our own culpability, indeed, in the face of this forgetting of the *mea culpa*, the artist receives an invitation that a sinner can't refuse. "It's almost like salvation/it's almost like the blues." There is no salvation apart from the blues. You see, while the blues name the pain, they invariably point towards healing. The blues do not shrink from our sinfulness, but they remain rooted enough in gospel to point to forgiveness.

Eschewing both a self-confident atheism and the cowardly averting of our gaze from the brokenness of the world and our own sinfulness, we have seen that Cohen consistently turns to prayer. If you've heard the invitation that a sinner can't refuse, where else would you turn? This is a short litany adapted from Psalm 45 in Cohen's *Book of Mercy*.

NOT KNOWING WHERE TO GO

Let us pray.

> Not knowing where to go,
> *I go to you.*
>
> Not knowing where to turn,
> *I turn to you.*
>
> Not knowing what to hold,
> *I bind myself to you.*
>
> Having lost my way,
> *I make my way to you.*
>
> Having soiled my heart,
> *I lift my heart to you.*
>
> Having wasted my days,
> *I bring the heap to you.*
>
> Blocked by every thought,
> *I fly on the wisp of remembrance.*
>
> Defeated by silence,

here is a place where the silence is more subtle.

And here is the opening in defeat.
And here is the clasp of the will.

And here is the fear of you.
And here is the fastening of mercy.

Blessed are you,
in this moment.

Blessed are you,
whose presence illuminates outrageous evil.

Blessed are you,
who brings chains out of darkness.

Blessed are you,
who waits in the world.

Blessed are you,
whose name is in the world.

COMING TO THE TABLE

For almost twenty years I served as the pastor to a worshipping community at the University of Toronto called Wine Before Breakfast. In this early morning eucharistic community we played a lot of Leonard Cohen, and we practiced a radically open table. The only criterion for coming to the communion table was hunger. Folks who were not sure whether they believed, who had either no experience with such a Christian community, or who were deeply disaffected and alienated from a prior Christian faith tradition, wondered whether the Eucharist was for them. They would ask, "If I don't understand, or maybe don't believe yet, is it okay for me to come to the Eucharist? Should I receive the bread and the wine?" And I would always reply, "Are you hungry?" "Are you here with the kind of hunger that you think a piece of bread and a sip of wine might begin to satisfy?" Invariably, the answer was "Yes." "Then you better come and eat," I would reply. "The table is set." I think that Leonard Cohen embraced such a welcoming spirituality precisely because he understood such hunger.

In chapter 2 of this book we discussed Cohen's wonderful depiction of covenantal dialogue and argument in his song "Lover, Lover, Lover." On the album *Field Commander Cohen Live*, there is an alternative final verse to that song that evokes the kind of radical welcome that is at the heart of a biblical landscape of faith:

> You may come to me in happiness
> Or you may come to me in grief
> You may come to me in your deepest faith
> Or you may come in disbelief

This is a priestly invitation. This is an altar call in the deepest sense of the word. In these lines there is an invitation to come to the altar where forgiveness is on offer. Whether your life is filled with a joyful faith or caught in grief and disbelief, the invitation remains. This is, if you will, a call to the table that has been set for all. With prophetic resonances, these lines engage in a priestly ministry that invites all who are hungry to a living faith.

REVISITING THE PRIESTLY CALL

In the very pathos of "Lover, Lover, Lover" we meet a living spirituality. This is no curatorship of a religious museum of fossils or a pile of dry bones. So it is not surprising that after some years of reflection and maturing, Cohen rethought his controversial 1964 "Loneliness and History" lecture at the Jewish Public Library. In a 1990 interview he said:

> Community is a lot more fragile than I understood then, and a lot more valuable, and to undertake the defence of a community is a high call and in no sense a betrayal of a personal destiny. That is more my position today, I would say. But I was a young man then, confronting, I suppose, the same problems as A. M. Klein, but choosing a radically different path than A. M. Klein had chosen.[2]

It seems to me that the abrasiveness of Cohen's 1964 lecture wasn't just a matter of the brashness of a young man, but of his struggle with his own sense of a priestly calling. Cohen was convinced that a priesthood of communal legitimacy and comfortable accommodation was palliative care of the tradition at best and museum curatorship at worst. Either way, such a priestly practice was in fact the abandonment of faith. Nonetheless, from a very early age, it would appear that Cohen knew that he wanted to live up to his name. To be a Cohen is to be born into a priestly line in Judaism. The name "Cohen" literally means "priest." In a 1983 interview he said:

> When they told me I was a Kohayn (*Kō-een*), I believed it . . . I didn't think this was some auxiliary information. I believed. I wanted to wear white clothes, and to go into the Holy of Holies, and to negotiate with the deepest resources of my soul. So I took the whole thing seriously. I was this little kid, and whatever they told me in

2. Cited by Mesic, "Priest of a Catacomb Religion," 34.

> these matters, it resonated. I wanted to be that figure who sang, "This is a Tree of Life; all that you hold onto." So I tried to be that. I tried to become that. That world seemed open to me. And I was able to become that . . . . That kind of thing sent a chill down my back. I wanted to be that one who lifted up the Torah. I wanted to say that. I wanted to be in that position.[3]

And that, many of us will testify, was precisely the position that Leonard Cohen took up in our culture. While always imperfect, never delivering a perfect offering, in many ways Cohen lived up to his name as a Kohayn through his poetry and music.

A PRIEST IN THE SHADOW OF AUSCHWITZ

There is, of course, no viable priesthood, no Jewish spirituality, no deepening of covenant in the context of our history apart from the Holocaust, apart from Auschwitz. It is, therefore, significant that throughout the last period of his career, Cohen usually opened his concerts with "Dance Me to the End of Love."

> Dance me to your beauty with a burning violin
> Dance me through the panic till I'm gathered safely in
> Lift me like an olive branch and be my homeward
>   dove
> Dance me to the end of love

First released in 1984 on *Various Positions*, this song takes its inspiration from Auschwitz. At this death camp in Poland, the Nazis assembled a small orchestra from the camp population to play as fellow Jews were unloaded

---

3. "I'm the Little Jew Who wrote the Bible." Interview with Arthur Kurzweil, in Burger, *Cohen on Cohen*, 383.

IF IT BE YOUR WILL

from the train cars and taken to the gas chambers and the furnaces. The musicians were forced to play or join the others in death. Cohen evocatively likens this performance as a dance to the end of love. This is a dance to the end. The end of everything. The end of any love. This is an ending in panic, where love is choked, snuffed out by Zyklon B gas, and burned in the flames of the furnaces. This is the end of all dreams in a nightmare of horror.

And yet the song does not leave us in despair. Cohen refuses to allow the horror of Auschwitz to have the last word. This is a dance "through the panic" to a place where we are "gathered safely in." In the face of such violence, the poet/priest imagines an ingathering, a homecoming. This is not a dance of defeat, but of resistance, even of hope. In the face of the catastrophic ending toward which this dance leads, Cohen has the audacity to insist that this is a wedding dance.

> Dance me to the wedding now, dance me on and on
> Dance me very tenderly and dance me very long
> We're both of us beneath our love, we're both of us above
> Dance me to the end of love

Here the burning violin is playing a dance that is truly to the "end" of love, the end to which love directs us, the end which is the telos of love. In the face of brutality this is a dance of beauty and tenderness.

> Dance me to the children who are asking to be born
> Dance me through the curtains that our kisses have outworn
> Raise a tent of shelter now, though every thread is torn
> Dance me to the end of love

While the horrors of genocide seek to eradicate a whole people, this is a dance of a new generation, a dance to the children who are asking to be born even in the face of such death. This is a dance of sexual intimacy and homemaking.

The end of love will "raise a tent of shelter now, though every thread is torn." By evoking Sukkot, the Feast of Booths, Cohen places Auschwitz in the exodus tradition of Israel. This too is a devastating wilderness on the pilgrimage to covenantal liberation. Like the Israelites living in tents or booths during their forty-year sojourn in the wilderness, so does the poet invite them, invite all of us, to raise a tent of shelter in the midst of the present wilderness "though every thread is torn." This is a spirituality devoid of sentimentality. This is no happy camping trip, or erecting cozy tents in the backyard, or at the synagogue for Sukkot. No, this is a tent that provides the barest of shelter through its torn threads. But we must raise it nonetheless, as an act of radical hope and resistance.

As a dove with an olive branch in its beak was a sign of homecoming for Noah after the flood, so the singer dares to hope for a homeward dove in the very first verse of the song. "Lift me like an olive branch and be my homeward dove." In the face of this ingathering unto death, this genocide that was also by nature a domicide—a murder of home—the priestly voice is called to sing of home, of an ingathering unto liberation, return from exile, and children waiting to be born.

There is no healing apart from pain. There is no homecoming apart from exile. There is no dancing to the end of love except through the fires of history. Sometimes the priest can sing in the face of the horror with a call to dance to the end of love. Sometimes the priest can sing of return, of homecoming, of an impossible hope in the face of it all. But there is no homecoming without grief, there is no hope without lament, and there is no faith without disbelief. The priestly call is to embrace that grief, lament, and disbelief on behalf of the community.

TELL ME THAT YOU LOVE ME THEN

Cohen was not done with the Holocaust after "Dance Me to the End of Love." Having danced through Auschwitz to the end of love, Cohen confronted God anew some eighteen years later in "Amen," on the 2012 album *Old Ideas*.

> Tell me again
> When I'm clean and I'm sober
> Tell me again
> When I've seen through the horror
> Tell me again
> Tell me over and over
> Tell me that you love me then

Within the landscape of a biblical imagination, to dance to the end of love is to dance with the covenantal God who both creates and redeems in love. And so, in what appears to be the absence of that love, having come through the horror of the Holocaust, the poet/priest comes before the Holy One and, on behalf of the community, raises his complaint by daring this God to say it again. "Tell me that you love me then." With the horror still piercing our souls, does the Holy One dare to repeat the covenantal invitation of love?

Priests who are unable to lament and do not have the courage to talk back to God are of no use to a living faith and no use to a grieving community.

> Tell me again
> When I've been to the river
> And I've taken the edge off my thirst
> Tell me again
> We're alone and I'm listening
> I'm listening so hard that it hurts

We are a people of the Word of words. We are a people constituted by listening. And so the poet addresses this God of the Word, this God of Torah. Lord, we are listening, "listening so hard that it hurts." So tell us again when we're "clean" and "sober," after we've stopped trying to deaden our trauma with alcohol, after we've "been through the horror." When the victims are singing in remorse and our thoughts are consumed with vengeance, when "the angels are panting/and scratching at the door to come in," what does the Holy One have to say then? When "the filth of the butcher/is washed in the blood of the lamb," and "when the rest of the culture/has passed through the Eye of the Camp," tell us again, Holy One, tell us again, the Great I Am, tell us again, Covenant Maker, tell us that you love us then. In the face of all of the evidence, in the face of our inconsolable loss, in the face of our broken hearts, tell us again that we are beloved.

A covenantal spirituality cannot be sustained apart from such abrasive complaint, such brutally honest lament before the Holy One. In the absence of lament we are left with an absolute deity, far removed from our pain, a distantly sovereign, apathetic, and uninterested god, untouched by pain. Such a distant God does not inhabit a biblical landscape. This is not the covenantal God of biblical faith. Precisely because the Holy One is a God-in-relation, a God of covenant, the psalmists can raise their cry, "How long, O Lord, will you hide your face?" (Psalm 13:1), and "Why, O Lord, do you stand far off? Why do you hide yourself in times of trouble?" (Psalm 10:1) The psalmists dare to accuse: "You have rejected and abased us." "You have sold your people for a trifle." "Because of you we are being killed all day long, and accounted as sheep for the slaughter" (Psalm 44:9,12, 22). Because God is in relation, because God is the one who responds to their cries, Israel does not shrink back from calling God to account in the face of their calamities. Indeed, for Israel to abstain from such lament, for Israel to remain in a polite piety of praise, devoid of complaint, would be for Israel to abandon the messy dynamics of a covenantal faith.

What is true of the prayers of Israel found in the Psalms is true of the voice of Israel in the prophetic tradition, especially during the exile. Consider the painful lament of Habakkuk.

> O Lord, how long shall I cry for help,
> and you will not listen?
> Or cry to you, "Violence!"
> and you will not save?
> Why do you make me see wrongdoing
> and look at trouble?
> Destruction and violence are before me;
> strife and contention arise.
> So the law becomes slack
> and justice never prevails.
> The wicked surround the righteous,
> therefore judgement comes forth perverted.
> (Habakkuk 1:1–4)

If God is not listening, if the Torah has no binding, if there is no justice, then how can covenantal faith be sustained? No wonder,

> The roads to Zion mourn,
> for no one comes to the festivals;
> all her gates are desolate,

> her priests groan,
> her young girls grieve,
> and her lot is bitter (Lamentations 1:4).
>
> Is it nothing to you, all you who pass by?
> Look and see
> if there is any sorrow like my sorrow,
> which was brought upon me,
> which the Lord inflicted
> on the day of his fierce anger (Lamentations 1:12).
>
> For these things I weep,
> my eyes flow with tears;
> for a comforter is far from me,
> one to revive my courage;
> my children are desolate,
> for the enemy has prevailed (Lamentations 1:16).

There is no one to comfort. Both the prophetic and the priestly voice agree, and both know that faithfulness requires an honest spirituality of lament that names the reality of the community in all of its horror, abuse, and disappointment.

Tell me again, cries the poet. Tell us again, laments the community. Tell us again, when we have no comforter, when all joy has reached its eventide and tears are our only food, day and night. Tell us again, when we are wracked in sorrow and there is no comforter near. But the audacity of the complaint is matched by the audacity of the reply, as the Holy One dares to answer, dares to tell Israel again of her place in the covenant.

> Here is my servant, whom I uphold,
>   my chosen, in whom my soul delights;
> I have put my spirit upon him;
>   he will bring forth justice to the nations.
> He will not cry or lift up his voice,

>   or make it heard in the street;
> a bruised reed he will not break,
>   and a dimly burning wick he will not quench;
>   he will faithfully bring forth justice.
> He will not grow faint or be crushed
>   until he has established justice in the earth;
>   and the coastlands wait for his teaching.
>
> See, the former things have come to pass,
>   and new things I now declare;
> before they spring forth,
>   I tell you of them.
>   (Isaiah 42:1–3, 9)

The prophetic voice and the priestly ministry of healing are never very far apart. And so Isaiah comes with a radical word of hope. In the midst of exile, homecoming. In the grip of fear, strength. In place of sorrow, joy. Instead of parched throats, living water. Bruised reeds will not be broken. Dimly burning wicks will not be quenched. This is music to the ears of fearful exiles whose throats are parched from wailing in lament. This is good news for dimly burning wicks about to lose all light or bruised reeds too broken to be of any further service. Burdened by horrific memories, having seen a devastating ending, the community hears a new word: "the former things have come to pass, and new things I now declare."

FROM THE OTHER SIDE OF SORROW AND DESPAIR

As if echoing Isaiah, Cohen brings a similar priestly greeting to his devastated community:

>   I greet you from the other side
>   of sorrow and despair

> With a love so vast and so shattered
> it can reach you anywhere.

So sings Cohen in the opening lines of "Heart with No Companion," on the remarkable *Various Positions* album. Sometimes it is hard to believe that there is another side of sorrow and despair. Nonetheless, the poet sings:

> And I sing this for the captain
> Whose ship has not been built
> For the mother in confusion
> Her cradle still unfilled
>
> For the heart with no companion
> For the soul without a king
> For the prima ballerina
> Who cannot dance to anything

When your life callings have been thwarted and you meet disappointment after disappointment, despair after despair, that is when the priest comes with a love that is the only engine of survival. This is a love that can bear the pain because it has gone through the horror and has found its true end, its deepest telos, on the other side of the furnaces. Precisely because this is a love that is shattered, broken, splintered, gassed, and crucified in human history, is it so vast, so expansive, so wide that it can reach us anywhere. In the face of crushing disappointment, of callings frustrated, empty cradles for confused mothers, unbuilt ships for captains of the sea, the loneliness of hearts with no companions, ballerinas who cannot dance us to the end of love, and souls without a king—that is to say, in the face of a sorrow and despair that is endemic to our times—Leonard Cohen wrote a country tune of repair, restoration, and return.

Not blinking from the "days of shame that are coming" or the "nights of wild distress" that are upon us, our priestly poet calls us to where only a Kohayn could call us: back to covenant. And in the spirit of that covenant he confesses, "Tho' your promise count for nothing/you must keep it nonetheless." Though our covenant-breaking past is well known, and all the evidence suggests that we are incurable promise-breakers, the poet calls us to keep covenant for the sake of those confused mothers, unfulfilled sailors, the lonely, the frustrated, the lost. Keep covenant, hold your promise, for the soul without a king. This is covenant-keeping for the sake of your neighbor, especially your broken and vulnerable neighbor.

Again, as confusing as it may be to the mainline music industry, we must recognize that Leonard Cohen is a post-secular poet. His witness is decidedly against modernist autonomy. Against a secular vision of life that can live without worship. Against a life without God, even if life with God is to be one of conflict, lament, and struggle. A "soul without a king" is a lost soul, without grounding, calling, or hope. And somehow we all know this to be true. It has always been an illusion to believe in autonomy. Secularism is not a religiously neutral vision of life, it is a religion itself. None of us lives alone, all of us need a vision, a goal, a higher calling. Deep at the heart of things, every soul needs a king. We may recoil at the colonial overtones of such language of royalty, not to mention the patriarchal resonances of such language, but the crucial thing that Leonard Cohen will not shrink from is that we are *homo religiosus* and *homo liturgicus*. We are incurably religious beings, creatures who live our lives in terms of ultimate loyalties, a sovereignty that grounds our lives.

And we are liturgical beings. We are creatures of worship, created for worship.

And we are *homo eroticus*. Our eros, our longing for intimacy, relationship, and home all finds its telos, its end, in God. No wonder Jesus said,

> Come unto me, all you that are weary
> and carrying heavy burdens,
> and I will give you rest.
>
> Take my yoke upon you,
> and learn from me;
> for I am gentle and humble in heart,
> and you will find rest for your souls.
>
> For my yoke is easy,
> and my burden is light. (Matthew 11:28–30)

Cohen is getting at the same thing by greeting us "from the other side/of sorrow and despair/with a love so vast and so shattered/it can reach you everywhere."

START AGAIN, I HEARD THEM SAY

The question is, how does that vast, yet shattered love reach us? Let me tell you a story.[4]

> It was early on the first day of the week,
> and it was dark.
> Much too early for a woman
> to be walking the streets alone,
> especially in light of all that had transpired.
>
> But Mary had to go.
> She simply couldn't wait any longer.

---

4. Based on John 20:1–18.

IF IT BE YOUR WILL

So she had to make her way out the city gates,
across the killing fields,
to the place where they had laid the body.

The vast love that she had met in him,
the hope, the healing, the forgiveness,
was now shattered.

But she had to go to the tomb.
Love required no less.

And what she saw crushed her.
Here was a cruel insult
heaped on top of her shattered heart.

The stone that had sealed the grave
was moved, and the body was gone.

So she ran.
She ran and ran and ran
until her lungs were about to burst.

She ran back to the others,
and in desperation,
she banged on that locked door.

"They have taken his body from the tomb,
and I don't know where they have laid him."

And so Peter and the other disciple ran.
They ran and ran and ran.

Still gasping for breath,
Mary ran after them.

And when she caught up with the men,
the look on their faces
only confirmed what she had feared.

RAGS OF LIGHT

He was gone.

The men didn't think to bring her home with them.
They didn't think that their sister might need some
    comfort.
They just left in their own despair.

So Mary wept.
She wept and wept and wept.

And then she looked into the tomb.
Maybe just to confirm her worst fear.

But the tomb wasn't empty!
Two angels were there.
How Peter had missed them,
no one knows.

"Woman, why are you weeping?"
asked one of the angels.

"They have taken away my Lord,
and I do not know where they have laid him,"
she choked through her sobbing.

Then, sensing someone behind her,
she turned around
and saw a man standing there.

He asked the same question as the angel,
"Woman, why are you weeping?"

And, supposing that this was the gardener,
she replied with boldness,
"Sir, if you have moved his body,
then tell me where you have laid him,
so I can go and take him away."

IF IT BE YOUR WILL

> And he said, "Mary."
>
> And in that naming,
> in that acknowledgment of who she was,
> Mary recognized that this was Jesus.
>
> In that naming she was greeted
> from the other side
> of sorrow and despair.
>
> Mary recognized that before her stood
> a love so vast and so shattered
> that it could reach her anywhere,
> even when things had all gone wrong.

What happens if we listen to Leonard Cohen's "Anthem," from the 1992 album *The Future*, in the context of this resurrection story from the twentieth chapter of the Gospel of John?

> The birds they sang
> At the break of day
> Start again
> I heard them say
> Don't dwell on what has passed away
> Or what is yet to be
>
> Ah, the wars they will be fought again
> The holy dove, she will be caught again
> Bought and sold, and bought again
> The dove is never free.

The birds may sing, but the dove is never free. It may be dawn, but it seems like nothing new is breaking forth. The wars will be fought again, while the holy dove "will be caught again/bought and sold, and bought again." There is a weary inevitability to it all. The "killers in high places" still "say their prayers out loud." They still seek divine sanction for their violence. The violence of Good Friday. The violence of homelessness, the refugee crisis, and geopolitical aggression. The violence of genocide. The violence of homo- and transphobia. The inherent violence of racism. The violence that our economic systems have imposed upon our planetary home. And, of course, all that violence summons up anger and prophetic judgment. Nonetheless, at the break of day the birds insist on bearing witness to the dawning of something new. "Start again/I heard them say/Don't dwell on what has passed away/or what is yet to be." If you have ears to hear, and if you can interpret this ornithological glossolalia—this bird speaking in tongues—then perhaps you can hear these birds discerning a new beginning in the face of tragic endings. It is almost as if these birds are quoting Isaiah:

> See, the former things have come to pass,
>   and new things I now declare;
> before they spring forth,
>   I tell you of them.
> (Isaiah 42:9)

Don't dwell on what has passed away; something new is dawning.

Moreover, this song has beautiful resonances with the Gospel of John. John is, after all, the Gospel of signs. "We asked for signs, the signs were sent." And here, at the end of it all, after the betrayals, after the holy dove has been captured once more, after the widowhood of a government that has crucified the Word of words, after the lawlessness of those who are bound to the Measure of all Measures, it all starts again. John begins with creation, and brings his story to a climax in new creation.

> In the beginning was the Word,

and the Word was with God,
and the Word was God.

All things came into being through him,
and without him not one thing
came into being.

What has come into being in him was life,
and the life was the light of all people.

The light shines in the darkness
and the darkness did not overcome it. (John 1:1, 3–5)

Echoing Genesis 1, John is retelling the story of creation in light of Jesus. And when it all comes crashing down, when it seems that the darkness has in fact overcome the light, indeed very early, on the first day of the week, while it was still dark, there is a crack, and light shines forth anew. What happens if we understand that crack to be the resurrection?

I've sometimes contrasted Cohen's "There is a crack in everything/that's how the light gets in" with Bruce Cockburn's "You've got to kick at the darkness until it bleeds daylight."[5] But now I'm not so sure that the two lines are so different. Yes, there is a militancy to Cockburn's song, in which there is no light unless we kick holes in the darkness, while Cohen's vision seems to be that there is always light behind the darkness, and that it is in the cracks, in the fissures of the world, the cracks in our lives, that the light gets in. We just have to find those cracks. But I wonder if those cracks are perhaps best understood as created by the power of life over death, the power of light that pierces the darkness. In other words,

---

5. Bruce Cockburn, "Lovers in a Dangerous Time," *Stealing Fire* (1984).

the darkness cannot overcome the light, and the resurrection is proof of that. In resurrection, Jesus breaks the bonds of death and the stone that would encompass the light in darkness is pushed aside, creating the crack in everything. That's how the light gets in. Or perhaps, that's how the light gets out.

It is the first day of the week. It is the day of creation. John is clearly circling back to the beginning of the Gospel, to the beginning which is creation. And here, at the end, in the darkness, before there is light, we have a woman in a garden, who meets a man that she supposes to be the gardener. Within the landscape of the biblical imagination, it is an honest mistake because the risen Jesus *is* the Gardener. Here is the New Adam, the Gardener of the New Creation. So . . .

> Ring the bells that still can ring
> Forget your perfect offering
> There is a crack, a crack in everything
> That's how the light gets in

There is no perfect offering. Indeed, perfection is the enemy of holiness. Perfection will always hold you back. Perfection will always paralyze you. If you seek perfection, then you will never have the permission to ring those bells. Perfection will end up leaving you with no offering at all. So, forget your perfect offering, and see the light that darkness cannot overcome breaking through the cracks. But don't think that this light will magically solve all the problems. Don't think that somehow in this light we are going to get it all together. After all, "You can add up the parts/But you won't have the sum." No, that would be the old arrogance that will only attempt to shut out light all over again.

And don't think that this new beginning, this resolution of all of our problems, is something that we can achieve, yet another accomplishment of human progress. "You can add up the parts/But you won't have the sum/You can strike up the march/On your little broken drum." There is no marching off to victory here. There is no heroic winning of the war that is at the heart of all things. No, our poet has something much more profound for us, something that leads us beyond autonomous control. Let's put the whole verse together:

> You can add up the parts
> But you won't have the sum
> You can strike up the march
> On your little broken drum
> Every heart, every heart
> To love will come
> But like a refugee

In this conflict, the light is only received as a gift of love. You see, "every heart, every heart/to love will come/but like a refugee." In this war at the very heart of our conflicted lives, the only path to new creation, the only way to see the light shining through the cracks in everything is that every heart comes home to love, comes home to the love which birthed us, comes home to the love of the Holy One, permeating all of creation. But we come home like a refugee, having lost everything. This is a new home in the face of our deep homelessness.

What an evocative image. Our hearts must come to love, but only as refugees, displaced from our home in Love. There is no coming home with perfect gifts, there is no coming home apart from new creation, there is no coming home apart from the light shining through the cracks, there is no coming home apart from resurrection, and there is no coming home without love. But this love is not some kind of victory march. Cohen offers us no triumphal songs of arrival. No, if we are to sing, and our priests should always encourage us to sing, then our song will be of a love so vast and shattered that it can reach into the deepest places of our brokenness. Such a love "is not some kind of victory march/no, it's a cold and it's a very broken Hallelujah."

A VERY BROKEN HALLELUJAH

At the very end of the informative documentary *Hallelujah: Leonard Cohen, A Journey, A Song*, we hear Cohen say, "You look around and you see a world that is impenetrable, that cannot be made sense of. You either raise your fist or you say, 'hallelujah.' I've tried to do both." In another interview he observed that "this world is full of conflict and full of things that cannot be reconciled, but there are moments when we can transcend the dualistic system and reconcile and embrace the whole mess, and that's what I mean by 'Hallelujah.'"[6]

It is not an overstatement to say that Cohen's "Hallelujah" has resonated more than any other song at the end of modernity. "Hallelujah" is a post-secular hymn. There is something deep in the human soul that wants to sing "Hallelujah" even if we don't understand that this is singing praise to God. Of course the song interweaves piety and sexuality. As we have seen, the two have never been separable. They are both expressions of *eros*. Regardless of whether it is in the climax of sexual intimacy or deep in the heart of prayer, human life is at its most authentic

---

6. Cited by Light, *Holy or the Broken*, 30–31.

when every "breath we draw is Hallelujah."[7] However, offering our hallelujahs has never been easy or without tension. Whether we are remembering the voice of the ancient psalmists or we are singing in our own post-secular confusion, these are always cold and broken hallelujahs.

The song recalls moments of intimacy when the communication lines were open, but then there was a fissure, a break. "There was a time you let me know/what's really going on below/but now you never show it to me, do you?" But that fissure is all the more pronounced because of the memory of union. "I remember when I moved in you/And the holy dove, she was moving too/And every single breath that we drew was Hallelujah!" Even though we know that the holy dove is bought and sold and bought again; even though we know that the holy dove is never free, nonetheless there is a memory, a covenantal memory, perhaps a memory at the foundation of all memory, of when the holy dove was moving in our midst, and every breath we drew was Hallelujah. Admittedly, such memories of love, revelation, and covenantal intimacy can fade, and we can become bitter in our loss. But this is neither a song of lament, nor is it a praise song. It lies somewhere in between.

> But it's not a complaint
> that you hear tonight,
> it's not the laughter of someone
> who claims to have seen the light,
> no, it's is a cold and a very lonely Hallelujah.[8]

This is a song of truth-telling. The artist "didn't come all this way just to fool you." This is the kind of truth that

---

7. Cohen, *Stranger Music,* 347–48.
8. Lyrics from the 1988 tour, *Cohen Live,* 1994.

people long for in a post-truth culture; a moment of authenticity in a culture of artifice and pretense.

There are, of course, hundreds of covers of "Hallelujah." At one point in 2008 the song held three places on the UK top forty. But I confess that I have never thought that anyone performed the song better than Cohen himself. Indeed, I think that the rendering of the song that Cohen performed on the 1988 tour tops them all. Employing alternative verses to the original recording (dropping the first two verses about David and then Samson), what I love about this particular performance is a powerfully climactic silence in the second-last singing of the chorus. After confessing, "And even though it all went wrong/I'll stand before the Lord of Song/with nothing on my tongue but Hallelujah," the chorus builds to a crescendo in which Cohen and backup singers Julia Christensen and Perla Batalla sing a culminating "Hallelujah!" and there is a three-second silence before proceeding with the hallelujahs that complete the chorus. That punctuation, that silence left to hang for a couple of seconds, musically captures the pathos, the longing, indeed, the eros of this amazing song.

If "there is a crack in everything/that's how the light gets in" was something of a credo for Cohen, and if "Born in Chains" was the statement of faith that he labored the longest to get right, then we could say that the "Hallelujah hymn" was, in a profound way, the only song he ever had. Or so confessed our poet/priest in his 2014 song "You Got Me Singing," on the *Popular Problems* album.

> You got me singing
> Even tho' the news is bad
> You got me singing
> The only song I ever had

> You got me singing
> Ever since the river died
> You got me thinking
> Of the places we could hide.

Here is a hymn about a hymn. Here is the artist, late in life, saying that there really only was one song that encapsulated them all, one song that got to the heart of his faith, one song that reverberated across the biblical landscape of the imagination.

> You got me singing
> Even though the world is gone
> You got me thinking
> I'd like to carry on
> You got me singing
> Even tho' it all looks grim
> You got me singing
> The Hallelujah hymn

Even though the news is bad. Even though the world is gone. Even though it all looks grim. Here we have a resilient faith against the odds. A faith for a culture in collapse. A faith when the center does not hold. A faith in the face of the dissolution of all that one held to be secure. Again, Cohen sounds like the prophet Habakkuk:

> Though the fig tree does not bud
>   and there are no grapes on the vines,
> though the olive crop fails
>   and the fields produce no food . . .
> yet I will rejoice in the Lord,
>   I will be joyful in God my Saviour. (Habakkuk 3:17–18)

The prophecy of Habakkuk ends with the same kind of "even though" we find in Cohen. Even though the world is in crisis and we are lost in exile. Even though it all looks grim in an agricultural collapse in which the fig tree does not blossom nor have the vines produced a crop of grapes. Even though it all went wrong, the olive crop is destroyed and the bloodied fields produce no food. Even though nothing holds and it is all coming apart, Habakkuk says, "I will rejoice in the Lord, I will be joyful in God my Saviour." And perhaps Cohen not only read Habakkuk but also the inscription at the end of this book of prophecy: "To the Leader, with stringed instruments." Cohen and Habakkuk were prophets in the crisis, and they were told not just to speak their prophecy, but to sing it.[9] And, while they both tend to sing laments, they both tend to sing the blues, Leonard and Habakkuk together insist upon a stubborn, persistent, and faithful, "even though." That "even though" is a priestly turn. There may be environmental collapse, and the river has died. There may be a sense of apocalyptic cataclysm, and we're looking for a place to hide. But this poet/priest invites us to sing the only song he ever had, the only song that really mattered, that Hallelujah hymn. And, with priestly arms open wide, he invites us to sing this hymn "like a prisoner in the jail," knowing that the "pardon is in the mail." In solidarity with "those people of the past" and in hope that "our little love will last," Cohen sings, and it is infectious.

IN OUR RAGS OF LIGHT

To sing "hallelujah" when everything has gone wrong is to offer praise and thanksgiving with eyes wide open to the counter-evidence. Such a stubborn faithfulness is at the heart of spirituality in the biblical landscape. But

9. Walsh and the Wine Before Breakfast Commnity, *Habakkuk Before Breakfast*, 84–86.

sometimes we just don't have the heart to sing. Sometimes the darkness is so thick, the hurt so deep that we can't get enough breath into our lungs to make a sound. In the midst of such deep pathos, such profound loss, we wonder if this isn't a time for song but for silence. There is a time to speak and to sing and a time to remain silent. And so the poet/priest prays:

> If it be your will
> That I speak no more
> And my voice be still
> As it was before
> I will speak no more
> I shall abide until
> I am spoken for
> If it be your will

This is no perfunctory, "Lord willing." No, this is the question that Cohen, as priest, as prophet, as a wordsmith called to our service, must ask. And we all must ask. In this covenantal relationship, as souls who have a king, we do not arrogantly speak out of our own puffed up self-secure wisdom. Rather, we must speak when we are called. As with speech, so with song.

> If it be your will
> That a voice be true
> From this broken hill
> I will sing to you
> From this broken hill
> All your praises they shall ring
> If it be your will
> To let me sing

Within the landscape of biblical faith, if we are to sing, then it will be from a place of brokenness. Only from this broken hill can we sing; from Sinai of the broken tablets, from Golgotha of the broken body, from Zion of the broken covenant. Only from this broken hill can we sing our cold and very broken hallelujahs. And if we are to sing, then we do not sing alone. All of creation, sharing our brokenness and driven by the same covenantal love as the rest of us, will join the chorus.

> If it be your will
> If there is a choice
> Let the rivers fill
> Let the hills rejoice

And in that singing, when all of creation joins the choir, these songs of mercy will resonate all the way into the "burning hearts in hell."

> Let your mercy spill
> On all these burning hearts in hell
> If it be your will
> To make us well

Echoing the leper who said to Jesus, "Lord if you are willing, you can heal me and make me clean" (Matthew 8:2), Cohen's prayer asks a question while hoping for a certain answer. The leper hopes that it is the Lord's will that he be made whole. And whispering through this song the poet/priest longs to be able to speak and to sing anew in a way that breaks through the cacophony, even when there is little left to say. And so the song moves even more deeply into prayer:

> And draw us near
> And bind us tight
> All your children here
> In their rags of light
> In our rags of light
> All dressed to kill
> And end this night

> If it be your will

If the Holy One still desires our speech and our song, then we implore the Creator to draw us back into covenant. Draw us near, bind us tight. Bind us to your love. Bind us to your mercy.

Just as we have raised a tent of shelter though every thread is torn, so are we all here in our rags of light, all dressed to kill. The light which was called into being in that first Word of creation, the light in which we are clothed, is all tattered and torn while we're dressed to kill, dressed to impress, dressed for violence, dressed for the night. But we long for the day to end this night. We long for the light to shine through the cracks of our lives. We long for the sun to rise on a new creation morning. We long for resurrection. But there is no resurrection without death.

LOVE, IN THE END AS IN THE BEGINNING

On his last album before his death, *You Want It Darker*, as Cohen continues to struggle with his God and with Jesus, he approaches his death in gratitude for a life animated, held, and healed by love. In the unspeakably beautiful song "If I Didn't Have Your Love," the poet/priest confesses:

> If the sun would lose its light
> And we lived an endless night
> And there was nothing left that you could feel
> That's how it would be
> What my life would seem to me
> If I didn't have your love to make it real

When it all comes apart, when there seems to be no possibility of a resurrection dawn, and we are left in the numbness of anomie, it is only love that can make life real to us, because reality is born of the creative, generative, and overflowing love of the Holy One. Without love, there is endless night. Without love, the world is "swallowed up . . . without a trace."

> And if no leaves were on the tree
> And no water in the sea
> And the break of day had nothing to reveal
> That's how broken I would be
> What my life would seem to me
> If I didn't have your love to make it real

Without love, creation dissolves and the dawn has nothing to reveal. Without love, we are left in deep brokenness and there is no healing. Without love, the living world is rendered stone. Without love, there is no resurrection, no hope. And while our poet/priest has faced such hopelessness, such despair and dissolution with an eloquence that has resonated amongst millions of us, in the end, he offers us this testimony to the healing, sustaining, and redeeming power of love.

Leonard Cohen never offered us a perfect offering. But the gifts that he brought were indeed gifts of wisdom, of prophecy, and of priestly healing. And I hope that he wouldn't mind me saying so, but these gifts are presented at a manger—they are gifts that keep pointing to Jesus.

Postscript
"You Want It Darker"

The first word was "light." There is no biblical landscape, there is no story to tell, there is no path to follow, or wisdom, or life, without light. "Let there be light" (Genesis 1:3) is the first word, the opening utterance of the Word of words. "And God saw that the light was good" (Genesis 1:4). There is no Measure of all Measures without light. That is why the psalmist declares, "Your word is a lamp to my feet and a light to my path" (Psalm 119:105). Within the imagination of a biblical landscape there is a metaphorical struggle between light and darkness. Echoing this first word, the prologue to the Gospel of John boldly proclaims Jesus as the Word from the beginning made flesh. And because of this Word, "the light shines in the darkness, and the darkness did not overcome it" (John 1:5). And in an act of imaginative, poetic, and theological audacity Jesus proclaims, "I am the light of the world. Whoever follows me will never walk in darkness but will have the light of life" (John 8:12).

Leonard Cohen was never quite convinced. Not about Jesus and not about light. We have already seen that on *You Want It Darker,* the last album before his death,

Cohen gives final voice to his struggle with Jesus in the song, "It Seemed the Better Way." But it is the title song from that album that brings his struggle with the light to its most eloquent and painful expression. Knowing that his life is coming to an end, the poet/priest refuses easy resolution or cheap spiritual acquiescence. The opening verse puts it all on the table.

> If you are the dealer
> I'm out of the game
> If you are the healer
> I'm broken and lame
> If thine is the glory
> Then mine must be the shame
> You want it darker
> We kill the flame[1]

Within the intense struggle of a covenantal relationship, one partner is declaring divorce. Within the biblical witness such a declaration of divorce usually comes from the side of the Holy One, but in this instance the final rupture and dissolution of the relationship is voiced by a human covenant partner.[2] If you are the dealer, if this gamble called life is somehow led by you and you are the one laying out the cards, then count me out. If you are the healer, if the Holy One comes with "healing in his wings" (Malachi 4:2), then it needs to be stated boldly and without hesitation that the human partner in this relationship remains deeply, deeply broken. And if the Holy One is shrouded in glory, then Cohen confesses that his must be the shame. This is a story of disappointment and betrayal. The One who said "let there be light" has demonstrated an uncanny attraction to darkness.

---

1. Using lyrics from *The Flame*, 143–44.
2. Cf. Hosea 2:1–13; 4:1–3.

POSTSCRIPT

"You Want It Darker" is not a question but an accusation and rebuke. As we have seen throughout this book, this kind of abrasive prayer is not uncommon within the landscape of biblical faith. Malka Simkovich puts it this way:

> As Cohen accuses God of causing human suffering, we must remember that Cohen is getting in on an existential debate that he knows has been ongoing since the biblical period itself, when Abraham argued with God, accusing Him of ruthlessness towards the people of Sodom, and Moses railed against God when He threatens to destroy the Israelites, and David beseeched God to stop causing him personal pain. Cohen, of course, is aware of this precedent, and sees himself as an extension of ancient voices who long ago asked questions that could not be answered.[3]

Is it abrasive to accuse the God of Light to be an agent of darkness? Yes, but that is the nature of biblical prayer, lament, and piety. This is not a spirituality of sentimentality but of struggle, argument, and sometimes accusation. Frankly, none of this should be unfamiliar to anyone who has been in a deeply committed intimate relationship. Arguments with our lovers are always the most painful.

Nor is this a scapegoating spirituality. Yes, the poet says to the Holy One "you want it darker," but then he immediately admits to a joint responsibility in that darkness. "We kill the flame." While the Holy One who is the light seems to be sovereign over a world of unspeakable darkness, that darkness has everything to do with human rebellion against the light. Again, the Gospel of John unpacks this dynamic with devastating clarity: "And this

3. Simkovich, "Wrestling with God."

is the judgement, that the light has come into the world, and people loved darkness rather than light because their deeds were evil. For all who do evil hate the light and do not come to the light so that their deeds may not be exposed" (John 3:18–19).

"We kill the flame." The pervasive darkness in which our poet/priest struggles, the insidious darkness that he identifies at the heart of the crisis of covenantal life, is a consequence of the killing of the flame. What flame might this be? Well, all we need to do is look at the cover of Cohen's final book, *The Flame*, in which this poem/song appears. There we see a green bush surrounded by the orange, red, and yellow flames of fire. This is, of course, the burning bush of Exodus: "The angel of the Lord appeared to [Moses] in a flame of fire out of a bush; he looked, and the bush was blazing, yet it was not consumed" (3:2). Here is the flame out of which came a Voice that called out, "Moses, Moses," to which Moses replied, "Hineni," "Here I am" (3:3). The word *hineni*, is on the tongue of only six people in reply to the divine call in the Bible: Abraham (Genesis 22:1, 7, 11), Jacob (Genesis 31:11; 46:2), Samuel (1 Samuel 3:4, 6, 8), Isaiah (6:8), Ananias (Acts 9:10), and, of course, Moses. And each time we hear the reply "hineni," each time that a biblical character replies with "Here I am" it is in response to a divine call by name. Each time, the Holy One speaks the name of the person being called. And each time, the response is not a simple acknowledgement that they have heard the Voice, but more poignantly they reply with "hineni," "here I am."

Cohen gives voice to his own "hineni" in "You Want It Darker." Three times, after accusing the Holy One of wanting it darker, the poet confesses, "Hineni, hineni/I'm ready my Lord." Asked about this at the launch of *You Want*

It Darker, Cohen described hineni as "that declaration of readiness no matter what the outcome, that's a part of everyone's soul. We all are motivated by deep impulses and deep appetites to serve, even though we may not be able to locate that which we are willing to serve." He went on to explain, "So, this is just a part of my nature, and I think everybody else's nature, to offer oneself at the moment, at the critical moment when the emergency becomes articulate. It's only when the emergency becomes articulate that we can locate that willingness to serve."[4] When the emergency becomes articulate. Isn't that what Cohen has done throughout his whole career? Bringing the emergency of our souls, the emergencies of our culture, the emergency of broken covenant to eloquent, allusive, and devastating articulation. And in that articulation, in that naming of our brokenness, the poet/priest lays our complaint before the throne of the Holy One, identifies the human complicity in the crisis, and most amazingly, retains a stance of surrender, devotion, and service to the Covenant God.

Moreover, the impulse to say "hineni," the motivation to serve, indeed the longing of the soul for a king, is not a curious propensity of the religiously inclined. This is not a Leonard Cohen thing, nor simply a Jewish thing. Rather, in that last interview, Cohen gently suggested that everyone is "motivated by deep impulses and deep appetites to serve, even though we may not be able to locate that which we are willing to serve." We are all *homo religiosus* and *home liturgicus*. The longing to serve, to worship, to say "hineni" is simply the human condition.

Not surprisingly, this prayer of a song still lives in the shadow of the Holocaust. There were "a million candles burning/for the help that never came." "They're lining up

4. *You Want It Darker Launch Transcript,* 17.

the prisoners/The guards are taking aim." In contrast to the absolute evil of genocide, Cohen acknowledges that his own demons "were middle-class and tame." But in the end he confesses, "Hineni, hineni/I'm ready, my Lord." Ready to listen to the call. Ready to acknowledge that the Holy One calls him by name. Ready to face that Holy One in the journey beyond this life.

With death ever more closely on his horizon, Cohen offers the opening lines of the Kaddish, the Jewish prayer of blessing and doxology over the dead. "Magnified and sanctified/Be Thy Holy Name." The Name revealed in that burning bush, the Name that dare not be voiced, the great "I Am Who I Am" (Exodus 3:14), the Holy One who will be who he will be is magnified and sanctified before the death of his children. And Cohen alludes to this prayer in the face of his own death. But the next line evocatively transposes this Jewish prayer into a Christian telling of the story. "Vilified and crucified/In the human frame." When the Holy Name enters history, when the Word of words takes flesh, that is, when the Covenant God fully enters into the fray of violence and betrayal, the result is murder. What does the magnified and glorified Holy One look like in the midst of this relationship? Vilified and crucified. Why? Because we kill the flame.

At the burning bush Moses received his call. God had heard the cry of the people in their bondage and was going to make good on his promise of covenant land for his people. From that flame the Holy One is revealed as a God of liberation, a God whose realm and reign is alternative to that of Pharaoh's empire. And the Voice calls Moses to be God's agent in this liberation movement. To which Moses replied, "hineni." Moses's response to the Voice in the burning bush, though hesitant and halting, nonetheless is hineni. Here I am, present to your Word, submitting to your call. And at the end of his life Cohen offers the same confession, "Hineni, hineni/I am ready, my Lord."

Nonetheless, "we kill the flame." While the flame did not consume the bush, human history has been a long process of extinguishing that flame. By desecrating the holy ground of God's good creation, by closing our ears to the Word of words, by ignoring the Measure of all Measures, by killing God in our violence and arrogance, we have killed the flame. And we wonder why it has all got so much darker. It was from the midst of the flame that liberation was proclaimed and every genocide, every injustice seeks to quench that flame. It was from the midst of the flame that the Name was revealed and every knee that bows to idolatry, every assertion of human autonomy from the binding of covenant, desecrates and denies the Name. And we wonder why it has all got so much darker.

But in the end, accusation and surrender embrace, complaint and praise join hands, and the threat of divorce is resolved in the confession of hineni. "I am ready, my Lord," ready to go on in covenant with you. The question remains: is the Holy One ready to receive such a confession, such a renewed commitment to covenant with us? Once we have killed the flame and desecrated the Name, is the Covenant God prepared to forgo the divorce? Will the Creator God also pronounce hineni? The answer is, yes. Twice. And it will come as no surprise that the two times that God says hineni are found in the book of Isaiah. The Tree of Life translation captures the hineni well in Isaiah 43:18–19:

> Do not remember former things,
> nor consider things of the past.

> Here I am (hineni), doing a new thing;
> Now it is springing up—
>> do you not know about it?
> I will surely make a way in the desert,
>> rivers in the wasteland.

The past transgressions, infidelities, and idolatries, all that we have done to kill the flame, are not memories worth keeping. The Holy One is not bound by that past, but replies to the cry of humanity, the longing for a return from exile, the groaning of creation, the call for newness in the midst of the tired narrative of betrayal and brokenness, with "hineni." "Here I am," bringing newness and hope to my desolate people.

Again, in Isaiah 58:6–9a, the Lord says hineni.

> Is not this the fast that I choose:
>> to loose the bonds of injustice,
>> to undo the straps of the yoke,
> to let the oppressed go free,
>> and to break every yoke?
> Is it not to share your bread with the hungry
>> and bring the homeless poor into your house;
> when you see the naked, to cover them
>> and not to hide yourself from your own kin?
>
> Then your light shall break forth like the dawn,
>> and your healing shall spring up quickly;
> your vindicator shall go before you;
>> the glory of the Lord shall be your rear guard.
> Then you shall call, and the Lord will answer;
>> you shall cry for help, and he will say, "Here I am."
> (hineni)

Calling Israel to covenantal justice and liberation, reminding the people of the Torah call to set the oppressed free and to share their bread, insisting on the protection of the stranger, orphan, and widow in their midst, Isaiah evokes the exodus when the angel of the Lord went before them as their vindicator and protector, in a pillar of cloud by day and a pillar of fire by night. In the midst of such a new exodus, on the path to such a renewed covenant, the people will call upon the Name, and the Holy One will answer, "hineni," "here I am."

Had Cohen's grandfather, Solomon Klonitsky-Kline, brought the young Leonard's attention to these two divine hinenis when they studied Isaiah together? We don't know. But in "You Want It Darker" I think that we can hear God's hineni echoing in response to Cohen's.

While there is something profoundly personal and individual about responding to the call of God with hineni, it is not something that one ever does alone. A path of covenantal spirituality is never individualistic. Hineni can never be reduced to the individual's "personal relationship" with the Holy One. And so it is profoundly beautiful that the Leonard Cohen who had so upset the Montreal Jewish community as a young man by taking on the mantle of the prophet, invites that community to join him in singing his final hineni. "You Want It Darker" features the choir of Cohen's Montreal synagogue, Congregation Shaar Hashomayim, together with their cantor, Gideon Zelermyer, providing vocal texture and accompaniment as our poet/priest sings both the Kaddish and "Hineni, hineni/I'm ready, my Lord."

In an oft-quoted 1967 interview with Sandra Djwa, Cohen said, "Everyone has a sense that they are in their own capsule and the one that I have always been in, for want of a better word, is that of a cantor—a priest of a catacomb religion that is underground, just beginning, and I am one of the singers, one of the many, many priests, not by any means a high priest, but one of the creators of the liturgy that will create the church."[5]

A cantor, a priest, a creator of liturgy for a catacomb religion, a church no less. Harry Freedman describes Cohen as a *paytan*, "a scholarly musician and poet, a prayer leader imbued in the religious traditions with a profound knowledge of Bible and Talmudic lore."[6] This rings true. A biblical vision resonates throughout Cohen's songs and poems. But Freedman also concludes that Cohen's ambition to be a priest of a catacomb religion "didn't come to fruition."[7] I'm not so sure. Is there a new catacomb religion that has emerged out of Cohen's work? Thankfully, no. But, Cohen has undoubtedly been a liturgist for our time, a tour guide of the biblical landscape of faith, a cantor singing for all of us in our rags of light, a prophet in the ruins, and a priest who greets us "from the other side of sorrow and despair."

---

5. Sandra Djwa, "After the Wipeout, A Renewal," in Burger, ed., *Cohen on Cohen*, 11.

6. Freedman, *Leonard Cohen*, 245.

7. Freedman, *Leonard Cohen*, 245.

Discography of Leonard Cohen

1. STUDIO ALBUMS

Songs of Leonard Cohen. Produced by John Simon. Columbia, 1967.

Songs from a Room. Produced by Bob Johnson. Columbia, 1969.

Songs of Love and Hate. Produced by Bob Johnson. Columbia, 1971.

New Skin for the Old Ceremony. Produced by Leonard Cohen and John Lissauer. Columbia, 1974.

Death of a Ladies' Man. Produced by Phil Spector. Columbia, 1977.

Recent Songs. Produced by Leonard Cohen and Henry Lewry. Columbia, 1979.

Various Positions. Produced by John Lissauer. Columbia and Passport, 1984.

I'm Your Man. Produced by Leonard Cohen with Roscoe Beck, Michael Robidoux, and Jean-Michel Reusser. Columbia, 1988.

The Future. Produced by Leonard Cohen with Yoav Goren, Steve Lindsey, Leanne Unger, Rebecca De Mornay, and Bill Gin. Columbia, 1992.

Ten New Songs. Produced by Sharon Robinson. Columbia, 2001.

Dear Heather. Produced by Leonard Cohen with Henry Lewry, Sharon Robinson, Ed Sanders, Anjani Thomas, and Leanne Unger. Columbia, 2004.

Old Ideas. Produced by Patrick Leonard, Ed Sanders, Anjani Thomas, Dino Soldo, and Mark Vreeken. Columbia, 2012.

Popular Problems. Produced by Patrick Leonard. Columbia, 2014.

You Want It Darker. Produced by Adam Cohen and Patrick Leonard. Columbia, 2016.

Thanks for the Dance. Produced by Adam Cohen. Columbia, 2019.

2. LIVE ALBUMS

Live Songs. Produced by Bob Johnson. Columbia, 1973.

Cohen Live: Leonard Cohen in Concert. Produced by Leanne Unger and Bob Metzger. Columbia, 1994.

Field Commander Cohen: Tour of 1979. Produced by Leanne Unger. Columbia, 2001.

Live in London. Produced by Edward Sanders. Columbia, 2009.

Live at the Isle of Wight 1970. Produced by Steve Berkowitz. Columbia, 2009.

Songs from the Road. Produced by Edward Sanders. Columbia, 2010.

Live in Dublin. Produced by Edward Sanders. Columbia, 2014.

Films about Leonard Cohen

Hallelujah: Leonard Cohen, A Journey, A Song. Directed and Produced by Dan Geller and Dayna Goldfine. Sony, 2022.

Ladies and Gentleman . . . Mr. Leonard Cohen. Produced by Donald Brittain and John Kemeny. National Film Board, 1965.

Leonard Cohen: I'm Your Man. Produced by Lian Lunson, Mel Gibson, and Bruce Davey. Lionsgate, 2005.

Leonard Cohen: Tower of Song. Directed by Jack Bender. Unified Heart Film Productions, 2018.

Marianne and Leonard: Words of Love. Produced by Nick Broomfield, Kyle Gibbon, Shani Hinton, and Marc Hoeferlin. Roadside Attractions, 2019.

The Song of Leonard Cohen. Directed and produced by Harry Rasky. CBC, 1980.

Bibliography

Benazon, Michael. "Leonard Cohen of Montreal." Interview, *Matrix* 23 (Fall 1986).

Bilefsky, Dan. "Is Leonard Cohen the New Secular Saint of Montreal?" *The New York Times* (March 6, 2018).

Billingham, Peter, ed. *Spirituality and Desire in Leonard Cohen's Songs and Poems: Visions from the Tower of Song.* Newcastle upon Tyne, UK: Cambridge Scholars, 2017.

Bloch, Karen Lehrman. "Healing of the Spirit: The Genius of Leonard Cohen." *The Jewish Journal*, July 3, 2019. https://jewishjournal.com/cover_story/301044/healing-of-the-spirit-the-genius-of-leonard-cohen/.

Bouma-Prediger, Steven, and Brian J. Walsh. *Beyond Homelessness: Christian Faith in a Culture of Displacement.* 15th Anniversary ed. Grand Rapids: Eerdmans, 2023.

Burger, Jeff, ed. *Leonard Cohen on Leonard Cohen: Interviews and Encounters.* Chicago: Chicago Review, 2014.

Cohen, Doron B. "The Prayers of Leonard Cohen: If It Be Your Will." A lecture delivered at the Leonard Cohen Event, Amsterdam., August 14, 2016. https://www.leonardcohenfiles.com/doron-amsterdam.pdf.

Cohen, Leonard. *Book of Longing.* Toronto: McClelland & Stewart, 2006.

———. *Book of Mercy.* Toronto: McClelland & Stewart, 1984.

———. *The Energy of Slaves.* Toronto: McClelland & Stewart, 1972.

———. *The Flame: Poems and Selections from Notebooks.* Edited by Robert Faggen and Alexandra Pleshoyano. Toronto: McClelland & Stewart, 2018.

———. *Let Us Compare Mythologies.* Toronto: McClelland & Stewart, 1969. First published in Montreal by Contact, 1956.

———. *Stranger Music: Selected Poems and Songs.* Toronto: McClelland & Stewart, 1993.

Cox, Julian, and Jim Shedden, eds. *Leonard Cohen: Everybody Knows: Inside His Archive.* Toronto: Art Gallery of Ontario, 2022.

Coupe, Laurence. "Reading Song as Poem: Leonard Cohen's 'Suzanne.'" *Academia Letters,* July 2021, article 2333. https://laurencecoupe.co.uk/leonard-cohens-suzanne/.

Devlin, Jim. *Leonard Cohen: In His Own Words.* London: Omnibus, 1998.

Freedman, Harry. *Leonard Cohen and the Mystical Roots of Genius.* London: Bloomsbury Continuum, 2021.

Fretheim, Terrence. *The Suffering of God: An Old Testament Perspective.* Philadelphia: Fortress, 1989.

Girard, Philippe. *Leonard Cohen On a Wire.* Translated by Helge Dascher and Karen Houle. Montreal: Drawn and Quarterly, 2021.

Glazer, Aubrey L. "Leonard Cohen Lives When Something Like Religion Happens to the Heart." *Tikkun,* January 22, 2020. https://www.tikkun.org/leonard-cohen-lives-when-something-like-religion-happens-to-the-heart/

———. *Tangle of Matter & Ghost: Leonard Cohen's Post-Secular Songbook of Mysticism(s) Jewish & Beyond.* Brookline, MA: Academic Studies, 2017.

Holt, Jason, ed. *Leonard Cohen and Philosophy: Various Positions.* Chicago: Open Court, 2014.

Kornhaber, Spencer. "Leonard Cohen's Dark Wisdom." *The Atlantic,* November 11, 2016. https://www.theatlantic.com/entertainment/archive/2016/11/leonard-cohen-rip-lyrics-worldview-death-freedom/507398/.

Kubernik, Harvey. *Leonard Cohen: Everybody Knows.* Toronto: Monti Publishing and More, 2014.

la Terre, Adam. "An Interpretation of 'The Faith.'" https://www.leonardcohenforum.com/viewtopic.php?p=216578&sid=4a4bb4e2ad75dbea36e6e7d761d12e7f#p216578.

Leibovitz, Liel. *A Broken Hallelujah: Rock and Roll, Redemption, and the Life of Leonard Cohen.* New York: W. W. Norton, 2014.

Light, Alan. *The Holy or the Broken: Leonard Cohen, Jeff Buckley and the Unlikely Ascent of "Hallelujah."* New York: Atria, 2013.

Maltz, Judy. "The Extraordinary Israeli Story Behind Leonard Cohen's "Lover, Lover, Lover." *Haaretz,* November 11, 2016. https://www.haaretz.com/israel-news/culture/2016-11-11/ty-article/.premium/the-extraordinary-israeli-story-behind-leonard-cohens-lover-lover-lover/0000017f-db94-df62-a9ff-dfd778930000.

Mesic, Jiri. "Leonard Cohen, The Priest of a Catacomb Religion." *Moravian Journal of Literature and Film* 6.1 (Spring 2015) 29–47.

Middleton, J. Richard. *Abraham's Silence: The Binding of Isaac, The Suffering of Job, and How to Talk Back to God.* Grand Rapids: Baker Academic, 2021.

Mus, Francis. *The Demons of Leonard Cohen.* Ottawa: University of Ottawa Press, 2020.

Nadel, Ira B. *Various Positions: A Life of Leonard Cohen.* Toronto: Random House, 1996.

Nietzsche, Friedrich. *The Gay Science.* Translated by Walter Kaufmann. New York: Random House, 1974.

Pally, Marcia. *From the Broken Hill I Sing to You: God, Sex, and Politics in the Work of Leonard Cohen.* London: T. & T. Clark, 2021.

Raab, Christian. "Leonard Cohen's Biblical Vision: How the Light Gets in." *Commonweal Magazine,* April 27, 2017. https://www.commonwealmagazine.org/leonard-cohen%E2%80%99s-biblical-vision.

Remnick, David. "Leonard Cohen Makes it Darker." *The New Yorker,* October 10, 2016. https://www.newyorker.com/magazine/2016/10/17/leonard-cohen-makes-it-darker

Rose, Daniel. "The BEST: Leonard Cohen." Tradition Online, February 25, 2021. https://traditiononline.org/the-best-leonard-cohen/.

Rossman, Philipp. "Leonard Cohen, Philosopher." *Maynooth Philosophical Papers* 9 (2018) 1–20.

Scharen, Christian. *Broken Hallelujahs: Why Popular Music Matters to Those Seeking God.* Grand Rapids: Brazos, 2011.

———. *One Step Closer: Why U2 Matters to Those Seeking God.* Grand Rapids: Brazos, 2006.

Showalter, Allan. "Stellar Video." January 28, 2016. https://www.leonardcohen.com/stellar-video-born-in-chains.

Simkovich, Malka. "Wrestling with God: Leonard Cohen's You Want it Darker." The Lehrhaus, November 14, 2016. https://thelehrhaus.com/culture/wrestling-with-god-leonard-cohens-you-want-it-darker/.

Tourangeau, Catherine. Review of Chantal Ringuet and Gerard Rabinovitch, dir., *Les révolutions de Leonard Cohen* and Aubrey Glazer, *Tangle of Matter & Ghost: Leonard Cohen's Post-Secular Songbook of Mysticism(s) Jewish & Beyond. Canadian Jewish*

Studies/Études juives canadiennes 25 (2017). https://www.academia.edu/38779453/REVIEW_by_Catherine_Tourangeau

Walsh, Brian J., and the Wine Before Breakfast Community. *Habakkuk Before Breakfast: Liturgy, Lament, and Hope.* Eugene, OR: Cascade, 2019.

Walsh, Brian J. *Kicking at the Darkness: Bruce Cockburn and the Christian Imagination.* Grand Rapids: Brazos, 2011.

Wolfson, Elliot R. "New Jerusalem Glowing: Songs and Poems of Leonard Cohen in a Kabbalistic Key." https://www.themathesontrust.org/papers/judaism/wolfson-new_jerusalem_glowing.pdf.

Wolfson, Elliot R. "The Wisdom of Brokenness in Leonard Cohen's 'Come Healing': Mourning the poet, the troubador, the rabbi." *Tablet Magazine,* November 15, 2016. https://www.tabletmag.com/sections/arts-letters/articles/leonard-cohens-come-healing.

You Want It Darker Album Launch Transcript. Canadian Consulate, Los Angeles, October 13, 2016. https://www.leonardcohenfiles.com/darkerlaunchevent.pdf.

Song Index

Ain't no cure for love, xx, 18–20, 35
Almost like the blues, 114–116
Amen, 123–124
Anthem, 133–137

Born in chains, 54–57, 65, 101, 140
By the rivers dark, 107

Closing time, 107
Come healing, 22

Dance me to the end of love, xx, 6, 120–123
Democracy, 23n17, 46n17, 102–107,

Everybody knows, 86–89

First we take Manhattan, 38, 107

Going home, 64–69

Hallelujah, 138–140
Heart with no companion, 30n5, 128–129

Here it is, 18

If I didn't have your love, 145–146
If it be your will , xviii–xizx, 46, 46n16, 143–145
Is this what you wanted?, 18
It seemed the better way, xvii, 22–24, 70, 148

Lover, lover, lover, 61–64, 118–119

Show me the place, 20–22,
Steer your way, 108–112
Story of Isaac, 48–52,
Suzanne, xiii, xvii, 8–15, 15n9, 15n10, 19, 25, 36–39, 70, 113

The faith, 42–44
The future, 38n12, 55n20, 66n25, 96–102
The law, 58–60
The Land of Plenty, 18
There is a war, 80–81
Tower of Song, 94
Treaty, 25–27

What happens to the heart, 18

You got me singing, 140–142
You want it darker, 147–155

Poetry Index

All my news, 4–5, 67n26

Ballad, 14

Book of Mercy, 28
#1, 28–29, 30n3
#25, 92–93, 93n10
#41, 72–74
#43, 3
#45, 116–117
#48, 31–35

City Christ, 14n7

For Wilf and his house, 14

Isaiah, 82–83

Moving into a period, 90–92

Saviours, 14

Song of Patience, 14n7

Scripture Index

GENESIS

1	42, 45, 53
	135
1:1–2, 3	39
1:3	147
1:4	147
2	33
2:6	33n6
4:9–12	41
6	44
6:5–7	42
6:6	95
9:8–17	44
22	xiii, xiv, 48
22:1–3	47
22:1,7,11	150
22:18–33	48
25	53
31:11	150
46:2	150

EXODUS

2:23–25	53
3:2	150
3:3	150
3:14	152
31:18	111n22

DEUTERONOMY

5:15	58
7:19	58
19:14	111n22
30:15–20	95n12

JOSHUA

24:26–28	111n22

1 SAMUEL

3:4	150
6,8	150

PSALMS

10:1	125
13:1	124
22:1	27
33	42
33:4–9	40
44:9,12,22	125
119:105	147

SCRIPTURE INDEX

ISAIAH

2, 21, 74, 75, 86, 89, 92, 98, 102, 114, 128, 155

1:2–9	107n20
1:27	101
2:5–22	107n20
2:5-18	84
5:1–7	107n20
6:8	150
24:1–20	107n20
24:1-3	93
24:4-6	94
24:7-9	95
24:10	95
24:11	95
24:12	96
24:19-20	96
42:1–9	107n20
42:1–3, 9	127
42:5–9	107n21
42:9	134
43:18–19	xiii, 153
48:22	59
51:16	60
52:10	60
53:1-5	107n21
53:3-5	22
53:5	22
58:6–9a	xiii, 154
60:1–22	107n20
60:1-3	1
61:2	75n2
66:14	60

JEREMIAH XI, 98

7:4	63, 80
20:9	56
20:4-7	71n1
31:33	56
32:33–35	51

LAMENTATIONS

1:4	126
1:12	126
1:16	126

EZEKIEL 98

14:6	101
18:30	101
10	98
36	111

HOSEA

2:1–13	148n2
4:1–3	148n2

HABAKKUK

	142
1:1–4	125
3.17-18	141

MALACHI

4:2	148

MATTHEW

5:38-39	22
8:2	144
11:28–30	130
27:46	27

SCRIPTURE INDEX

MARK

1:14-15	101
16:3	21

LUKE

4:18-19	74
4:24	76
18:1–8	30n4
19:39–40	111n22
10:42	22

JOHN

1:1, 3-5	135
1:5	147
2:1-2	26
3:16	23
3:18–19	150
8:12	147
16:13	23
20	133
20:1–18	130n4
20:26–29	56n21

ACTS

9:10	150

REVELATION

	71
21:1-5	68

www.ingramcontent.com/pod-product-compliance
Lightning Source LLC
Chambersburg PA
CBHW032146160426
43197CB00008B/795